TRINITY
COLLEGE LONDON PRESS

C000097961

TEACHING NOTES

for Trinity College London
Piano exams 2018–2020

Initial–Grade 8

Written by
Pamela Lidiard
& Graham Fitch

Published by
Trinity College London Press
trinitycollege.com

Registered in England
Company no. 09726123

Printed in England by Halstan & Co Ltd., Amersham, Bucks

Contents

Authors

Pamela Lidiard is deputy head of keyboard studies at the Guildhall School of Music & Drama. As well as teaching and coaching pianists and singers, she also co-ordinates the postgraduate course for accompanists.

Graham Fitch maintains an international reputation as a pianist, teacher, writer and adjudicator. A regular contributor to *Pianist Magazine* and author of www.practisingthepiano.com, Graham runs a very busy private practice in London. He is a principal tutor on The Piano Teachers' Course (EPTA) UK and gives regular workshops and classes across the UK.

Introduction

These notes have been prepared for the benefit of teachers and students preparing for Trinity College London Piano exams using the 2018-2020 syllabus. There is of course no 'one' way to play any piece of music, and this holds good for exams just as much as for concert performances. Examiners will always be ready to accept many different ways of playing the pieces, so long as they are well prepared, carefully thought out and appropriate for the style of the music being performed.

From Initial to Grade 3 there is one list of pieces only, from which three pieces are freely chosen. From Grade 4 up to Grade 8 pieces are in two groups; two pieces are chosen from one group and one from the other. This arrangement allows candidates to play as much as possible of the music that they themselves enjoy and which shows off their skills in the best and most balanced way. As with all exam programmes, candidates should aim to demonstrate a variety of styles and techniques within their programme.

Marks are awarded separately to each piece for each of three main areas:

▶ fluency and accuracy: the ability to perform fluently, with a stable pulse and with an accurate realisation of the notation

▶ technical facility: the ability to control the instrument effectively, encompassing the various technical demands of the music

▶ communication and interpretation: the interpretation of the music and the way the performance conveys a sense of sylistic understanding and audience engagement.

Detailed criteria for assessing performances are published, and candidates and teachers should look carefully at those that relate to the grade being taken, to make sure that their preparation is focused correctly.

All pieces should be prepared in full unless otherwise stated; repeats should be omitted unless instructed otherwise. All *da capo* and *dal segno* instructions should be observed.

A final word of advice: enjoy practising and performing the pieces – your enjoyment will come across to the examiner and it will make the exam a happier event for everyone involved.

Key

A solid line denotes a piece within the Trinity music book for the grade.

A dotted line denotes a piece from the alternative list.

For pieces in the Trinity book for the grade, page numbers have been given.

Teachers may photocopy pages from this book to use with students.

Initial

At Initial, candidates will typically be able to show that they have acquired a basic foundation on their instrument; they will demonstrate some interpretation through variation in dynamics and articulation, with a limited variety of pace. They will perform audibly, with a sense of enthusiasm and enjoyment, and with some awareness of audience. These features will be demonstrated through material that is short enough to allow candidates at this level to maintain concentration through to the end. Content will be simple and straightforward, often with attractive titles relating to familiar subjects and contexts. The musical language will be simple and accessible.

Initial

Stahl   Stick and Hat (duet)   page 2

The added warmth and harmonic richness that comes with the addition of the secondo part transforms the simple primo. Secondo players could add in some subtle pedalling too, again to add warmth – despite its rather enigmatic title, this sounds more like a lullaby to me, fading into sleep in the final bars.

Most of this is self-explanatory. The dynamic levels are carefully marked, ensuring the part with the melodic interest projects most strongly. Get primo players to sing the secondo melody in the middle section as they play their accompaniment, both to keep those rocking crotchets steady, and to add shape to what is otherwise a rather uninteresting six bars. For the exam, there is no need to move up an octave for the chords in bars 19-20, but it is a nice effect in concert. Make sure pianists know exactly where they are going before they start to move position, and that secondo is aware that primo has a move to make, and a change of dynamic. Distances are often closer than we think – *look* at where you're going first, *then* move straight there. Easy!

Reinagle   Allegro (no. 4 from *24 Short and Easy Pieces*)   page 4

Although born in Britain, Alexander Reinagle made Philadelphia his home, where he had a private teaching practice as well as getting involved in many of the musical activities of the city. We primarily know him as a composer of teaching pieces and, although this is not the most inspiring choice at Initial level, it is solidly crafted and pedagogically sound.

In the central section, play the bass line *legato*, following the natural shape of stressed dominant resolving to tonic within the contrasting dynamic levels. It may be a little early to teach your pianists to conduct, but I find it useful to imagine how a conductor would direct the wind to play *forte*, then elicit a *piano* response from the strings – it needs a fraction more space than if both were to play *forte*. The pulse doesn't stop, but bends just enough for a different *piano* character and colour to be recognised and appreciated before returning to the confident, full *forte* tone.

Badings   Canon   page 5

This is quite a sophisticated little piece, despite its apparent simplicity. It requires independence from the two hands, which also implies an ability to hear two separate voices. All sorts of games can be played to help develop this: singing rounds of course, but also playing one line and singing another, playing as a duet and listening to spot a mistake in the teacher's part. Even getting pianists to talk to you while they play a scale gets different parts of the brain firing at once.

But even before that, it will be useful to play the theme here with both hands at the same time (ie beginning the LH one bar early). You can play the notes as written, a tantalising 7th apart, or move the LH to make it more consonant. Listen for the release of the fourth note, making it sound as natural as possible. Then play that phrase one hand after the other, listening to ensure they sound the same, then overlap as written. There you are – one of those essential pianist's skills that *probably* helps develop the brain for many other subjects as well!

Heumann   Spanish Guitar Player   page 6

An unusual piece, the flattened second providing the Spanish flavour. The slurs in the first section are ambiguous; they imply a releasing of the third crotchet, but I would suggest making the silence between the bars minimal. Each bar *diminuendos* from the downbeat accent, and this lightening of the last crotchet, releasing it just before the next accent, is enough to fulfil the demands of the slur. The central section has a contrasting mood, lyrical, gentler, more wistful perhaps. Listen for perfect synchronisation of the bass chords and enjoy the *crescendo* back to the more dark and upright opening music. Note that the two first time bars will not be played at all in the exam.

Harris   Spies on a Mission   page 7

There's relatively little material here; Paul Harris very cleverly places the same motifs within different surroundings. But don't be fooled – there's still a wealth of detail to incorporate into the performance. Having a story may help: confident swagger at the opening, seeing something that makes you suddenly more nervous at bar 5, pretending nothing at all happened in bar 9, but gradually slinking away at the end, until, BAM, a car backfires…

Articulation first. Ideally the crotchets in the thematic material should be longer than those marked *staccato* in the accompaniment in bar 9. Similarly the two-note slurs all end with a *staccato* quaver, but the three-note slurs finish on a crotchet, that will naturally be, if not a full crotchet's length, longer than the released quaver. Rhythm: it's easy to keep time on the second and third lines, against a regular crotchet pulse, but more tricky on the first and last lines. Don't think of the rests as empty time; hear the repeated crotchet chords in your head, or imagine an echo of what you've just played in the rest. Lastly, dynamics. Fairly straightforward, but remember that the accompanying chords should always be a little softer than the melodic material. Enormous fun – enjoy!

Béra-Tagrine   Conversation   page 8

This moves at an unhurried pace, but it is surely the right hand doing most of the talking? Perhaps the conversation is between the phrases, bar 2 agreeing with what was said by bar 1. A flexible wrist will allow the hand to adjust laterally as it moves from the thumb to the fifth finger, and to gently rise to release the third quaver. No exaggerated movements, but the *diminuendo* marking implies a passive, floating end to the three-note phrase, rather than the more active, definite *staccato* asked for in the last bar. The commas at the end of lines 2 and 3 are simply small breathing places, but shouldn't interrupt the even flow of the crotchet pulse. Plenty of articulation detail to work on – a brilliant brain workout as you practise maintaining the *legato* in one hand, while the other lifts. Try playing the final bass note with a finger 2 or 3 rather than 5, making it easier and safer to find and to accent. Try writing your own script for this conversation, make those dynamics come alive by putting real thoughts and feelings behind them.

Initial

Strecke The Waltz of the Toads page 9

The title is no doubt meant disparagingly, the grating seconds representing the croak of the toads. But there are fewer toads than there used to be, so it is good to have an opportunity to put them centre stage. This would be an excellent piece to teach by rote; whereas you could spend ten minutes getting a young pianist to read the notes of the chords, you could show them where they are on the piano much more quickly. I would use fingers 2 & 3 for all the seconds – the hand is well-balanced with that fingering – and save the thumb for the sixths. Listen for the release of the minims in the bass and avoid lifting the hand too far off the keys for the *staccato*. Staying close to the keys is safer and will probably produce a better sound. A delightful choice.

Charlton Tickery Tockery page 10

This sounds immediately attractive and fun, but Kay Charlton has packed it with detail to make it educational as well. There are several position changes, and a useful practice technique would be to find each position in turn, playing the first note or chord only. So the RH would play the first chord in bar 1, then move to the E in bar 4, then to the chord in bar 8, etc. Check that the wrist and arm stay supple, avoiding any tension as you plan and visualise each move in advance. Once the positions are well known, try finding them out of order: where is the RH in bar 9, bar 4, bar 13? This should be a fun game, the aim being to find ease in negotiating your way around the keyboard.

Play *legato* only where marked, otherwise slightly separate the crotchets, for instance in bars 2 & 3. Play the same phrases at different dynamic levels; how does *mf* feel and sound in comparison to *f*, to *ff*? Finally, the title suggests something clock-like, so be sure to keep that pulse absolutely steady, particularly during the rests. Two beats only for the final chord – feel that last rest firmly stopping the sound. Rests have power too!

Daxböck et al. Lullaby page 11

There are two main elements to this rather mesmerising lullaby: the rocking bass part and the smooth dotted rhythms in the melody. A little rotary motion will perhaps help the LH, keeping the movements small and the wrist flexible. You may like to practise the dotted rhythms in scales, keeping one hand on even crotchets, the other playing dotted crotchets and quavers. Try it both ways around, always listening for the quaver to be precisely in the middle of the two crotchets, maintaining the *legato*. Try singing the dotted rhythm against the LH crotchets, and then singing crotchets against the RH melody. All these games aim to allow beautifully smooth, bump-free, lyrical playing. When that is completely mastered, do also check that the melody is projecting more strongly in relation to the accompaniment in both dynamic levels. In the final bars remember that to play softer the notes need to go down more slowly. Keep the fingers close to the keys and feel the resistance as they depress...how slowly can you press the last notes and still have them sound enough to sustain for two beats and a pause?

Arnold Two Sad Hands *Queen's Temple*

This rather lovely piece, with its emphasis on *legato* and subtle phrasing detail, is perhaps not the easiest choice here, but one well worth playing. Plenty of hands separately practice first; feel the freedom in those wrists to help with the shaping of each phrase. Even when no dynamic changes are marked, as in the first phrases, they are still implicit: there's a natural sense of moving up to the top E and then relaxing the sound as you descend. Projecting the shape through dynamics is better

6

than being too pedantic about making a break in sound at the phrase ends when the mood is this quiet and gentle. Sometimes the hands shape together, but the challenging moment comes right at the start where they are in canon.

Dynamics are often a question of mood and colour: imagine a violin and viola duet at the opening, then maybe a richer clarinet and bassoon duo for the major *mp* section, returning to the strings for the final four bars. Encourage performers to find a way of getting into this 'sad' mood before they begin, making the link between music and expression right from the start. ♩ = c. 80.

Beyer   Lyrical Piece, op. 101 no. 39   *Kjos*

A bright tempo, around 132 crotchets per minute, is needed to allow the long four-bar melody to sing in one breath. Experiment with fingering for that first phrase: yes, the LH needs to stay in a five-finger position for its rocking accompaniment, but this can constrict the hand, and that opening phrase needs to be physically comfortable to achieve the lyricism demanded by the title. I like starting on 2, moving round and over for the last G. It's excellent training to play the melody by ear, rather than by fingers, so try various options and see which you agree feels and sounds best.

There are no dynamic markings on the score after the initial *mp*, but when you repeat the same music from bar 9, you may like to play it a little more quietly, making a *crescendo* on the last line, or a little more loudly, making a *diminuendo* on the last line. Notice that the last three notes in bar 8 link under one slur to the repeat of the opening. Finally, the LH. This provides ideal rotation practice, but be sure that the fingers are also rounded and active. Use a little more energy on the bass notes to make a counter-melody to the RH, and avoid heavy thumbs on the repeated Ds.

Crosland   King for a Day!   *Ferrum*

A bright C major is appropriate for this magisterial bass melody. Good to shine the spotlight on the LH for a change and this piece is perfect for working on a rich, full tone. Strong fingers, but with a flexible wrist; check there's no tension held there, instead feeling that each finger *releases* into the key – a very different sensation from *pressing* the key down. Notice the rest in the bass in bar 8, an opportunity to take a big breath before proclaiming a day off school. The accompanying chords in the RH play the part of the faithful retainer here, dynamically less prominent and detached. Listen for equality of length, not allowing the second chord to sustain for longer than the first. Not many musical subtleties here perhaps, but a useful *cantabile* exercise for the LH. Needless to say, 'King' can be crossed out and replaced by 'Queen'.

Gurlitt   Trumpet Tune   *Kjos*

The main interest here is in the RH trumpet melody, but it is worth spending some time on those LH chords. Feel the balance in the hand for each one; it will be most comfortable if it is angled slightly differently for each, towards the fifth finger for the open fifth, but more towards the thumb for the third. These small accommodating lateral wrist movements will allow perfect synchronisation of the notes, the arm always placed behind the hand. Practise these chords in the right dynamics too: strong, energised fingertips for *f*, and then a more cushioned feeling for the second line *mp*. Feel the gradual increase in energy, as you *crescendo* back to the vibrant *f*.

The top part is straightforward. A five-finger position is probably best, but check that the limited movement doesn't lead to any tension. Notice the difference between the second notes of bars 2 & 4: the G in bar 2 is a release at the end of the slur, whereas the *staccato* G in bar 4 is more active and definite in sound. Thinking in minims will help with the long phrase in line 3 and ♩ = c. 66 is a good tempo.

Heumann Harlequin Waltz *Schott*

This is fun to play, although it might take a while to get used to those wrong-sounding Bs! A five-finger position in both hands, with each four bars a variation on the Lydian motif. Keep the fifth finger well rounded and supported in the LH – no collapsing and playing on the side of the finger. Some co-ordination issues to practise when the waltz accompaniment plays *staccato* 2nd and 3rd beats, with the melody singing *legato* on top. I like to work at this away from the piano at first, taking notes out of the equation, just practising movements. Avoid lifting the fingers too high for *staccato*; see how close you can stay while listening to the sound stop. In reality, the finger doesn't need to leave the key at all.

The marked tempo is quite brisk, but necessary, and would make repeats possible in the exam, noting the *decrescendo* and *ritardando* in the last repeat.

Orff Tanzstück (Dancing Piece) *Schott*

Carl Orff may be best known for *Carmina Burana* but he was also a genuinely innovative and far-sighted music educator. This ostensibly straightforward piece is musically very satisfying and practises articulation, phrasing and dynamics. A tempo of around ♩ = 112 would suit well. Both the repeats and the DC should be observed.

We are clearly in G major for the first line, with a *legato* bass pitted against a dancing RH, combining *legato* and *staccato*. The commas at the end of each four bars signify a complete break in sound, but they should be incorporated into a regular pulse – otherwise those dancers will be confused. Both hands change position for the second line, which is built on the dominant of C. The mood here is more sturdy, the dancers heavier and even their *staccato* jumps less supple and elegant. I would suggest a good accent on the bass fifth both times, listening to ensure it really lasts for four bars, but also checking that you are not still pressing into the keys – very little weight is needed to keep them down. Then return to the lighter-footed, more nimble dancers of the first section, feeling a concomitant lightness in the arms.

Sebba Wotcha Doin'? *Trinity*

This will be a popular choice, but it's a tricky little piece, with oodles of detail squeezed into its ten bars. The presence of some slurs implies that notes without them are detached. The speed is fairly relaxed, so it allows time to detach the semiquaver as well as the dotted quaver in the first bar and elsewhere. Listen for the difference in bar 2 as the RH plays four separated notes answered by the LH's *legato*. Extreme dynamics, as asked for on the last line, can be overdone by young pianists. It is easy to make the *ff* hard and ugly, or the *pp* too insubstantial to project (mind you, these are problems for all of us), so careful listening to the sound will be needed. Remember that dynamics are to do with speed, the speed at which the note is depressed, so a very quick movement is needed for *ff*, not one that is over-pressed or tense. The title could relate to this last line perhaps, with a tentative question receiving a confident, boisterous reply: 'having my tea'.

Stahl Today I'm Fine (duet) *Breitkopf*

This has a cheerful mood and my spirit also lifts when I see a slightly more sophisticated accompaniment as here. You could encourage an older student to play secondo, making sure their dynamics are in relation to their partner's. Otherwise enjoy playing this one yourself! Lots of musical detail to assimilate, particularly the varying note lengths and the *crescendos* and *diminuendos* between dynamic levels. Yes, explain how you make notes sound louder or softer, but also check that your pianists are really listening. Play to them: which note was louder? Is this getting softer or stronger? Check posture too: we seem instinctively to make ourselves smaller to play *piano* – not necessary! Separate the bass minims equally in bars 1-4, avoiding holding the second one, and note that there is a missing slur in bars 3-4, which should surely be the same as bars 19-20. A few places where the two players have different note lengths, bar 8 for instance, and confident duos could ease into the recapitulation, bars 16-17. Definitely more challenging for both players than the other duet on offer here, but well worth it. A tempo that is a few notches below the marked 168 is acceptable, and the repeat is not necessary in the exam.

Strecke Ball Playing *Breitkopf*

I remember an exercise, perhaps a Dalcroze exercise, in which we had to throw a ball so that it would take either a crotchet, or a quaver, or a minim to reach our partners. Something similar is going on here, with the first 8 bars requiring a quick action on the first and second beats of each bar to release the notes *staccato*, whereas in the second section the RH has minims at the beginning of each bar, and the LH crotchets are small chords and no longer *staccato*. Interesting to feel the different energy and movement in the hands as they adjust to the differing articulations. Note too that the melody is not *legato* on the second line. Rather, the hand should slightly lift before each upbeat to observe the small phrase marks. Although there is just the one dynamic marking, find the high points of each phrase so that there is still a sense of shaping: perhaps towards the Eb in the first 4 bars, and later towards the F♯. Experiment with fingering too; the easy option is a five-finger position, but starting on 4 in the RH, and then shifting down a note on the F in bar 4, following a similar pattern in the second half, may lead to a more relaxed hand. ♩ = 160 is a good tempo.

Terzibaschitsch Interval Magic *Trinity*

This will be a good choice for many pianists. It practises developing a firm, round tone for the melody, synchronising small chords in the bass, and maintaining a smooth melodic line while the LH lifts for each new chord. Around ♩ = 108 will be ideal to achieve all these elements.

Playing that first third in the LH demands a well-supported little finger; you want the tips of both fingers resting on the notes so that when the hand pushes into the keys, always with a supple wrist, they both sound together. Try getting your pupil to listen to you playing chords, telling you when they synchronise and when the notes are fractionally apart. I would also suggest thinking of releasing the chord on the last beat of the bar, giving plenty of time to concentrate on keeping the melody *legato* and to prepare the next chord. Good to have the words to give shape to the phrases, but no singing in the exam please!

Terzibaschitsch Round Dance (duet) *Trinity*

The right hand sings two phrases alone, but elsewhere is doubled at the octave by the left hand, making this a relatively easy choice. There are changes of position, from C position to F position, and you could practise this shift without the music until it is easily found. Have you noticed how things are nearly always nearer than you think on the keyboard? The distances aren't really so great, yet we often exaggerate the difficulty in our minds! Once that shift of hand position is mastered, the rest should quickly follow. Use a good drop-float technique for the two-note slurs and find a natural shape to the melody within the *mf* dynamic. A small variation of tone colour would be possible in bar 25, perhaps starting this phrase a little less and making a *crescendo* to the end. This is a good tune to sing and move to, getting the feeling of movement and buoyancy that will achieve the 'dance' character asked for in the title. Try it at ♩ = 152.

| Wilton | Allegro moderato (1st movt from *Sonatina*) | *Kjos* |

All our more contemporary composers are wonderfully imaginative, but it is refreshing to find this simple, balanced, classical piece in the syllabus. Both hands stay in a C position throughout, but this is an opportunity to work on a rounded, comfortable hand position, making sure the little finger plays from the knuckle bridge and doesn't lean on its side, and that the thumb is not too flat and heavy. Listen to the balance between the hands – the bass notes need enough depth of sound to sustain their tone and support the melody, which will sing easily two octaves above. A crotchet speed of around 132 works well. Interestingly in other editions bar 12 is different and not an exact repeat of bar 10. Indeed, this was the case when this was an exam piece a few syllabuses ago, so do make sure you are playing from the correct edition for the current exam.

Grades 1–3

At Grades 1–3, candidates will typically be able to apply their knowledge, understanding and skills to produce a performance that demonstrates careful preparation, understanding and the beginning of thoughtful interpretation based on some creative engagement with the material. Candidates will perform clearly and accurately, with a fluent technical command appropriate to the level and a sense of spontaneity, sustaining these qualities through to the end. Through variations in pace, volume, rhythm and articulation they will be able to create and convey mood. These features will be demonstrated through material of sufficient length to allow candidates to show their ability to establish and sustain their performance and interpretation. Content will include easily recognisable styles (eg minuet, blues) as the foundation for the exploration of musical styles outside their immediate experience. The musical language will contain a variety of expression across the three pieces and will demand awareness of balance and phrase.

Grade 1

| Kirkby-Mason | Mango Walk (duet) | page 2 |

I can imagine that this will be a popular duet, with many pianists already knowing the catchy tune. I would take the opportunity to discuss chords I and V⁷, whose broken chords feature in several bars, either divided between the hands or hands together. Find the tonic triad and then its inversions, stopping on the second inversion. If you then play the first bar of the melody, can your student find the notes and rhythm for bar 2 using just the inversion of the triad? If they can work out the notes themselves, first RH, then LH, then divided between the hands, this will make remembering what happens in bars 2, 4, 6, 8, etc so much easier. We remember what we understand. You can play a similar game with V⁷. An alternative fingering for the beginning would be 3 on the D, using 1, 4 on the B, C on the sixth & seventh quavers.

A note about the pauses: one of the players will need to lead the release of these chords, and you could try it both ways. But the mood is upbeat, fun, so the pause doesn't want to be so long that it fades into *p*, but rather wants to release with energy, almost with a flourish at the end. So time the pause so that the drive of the *crescendo* takes you all the way into the rest. It's tricky to synchronise the last bar with the arpeggiated chord in secondo, so a little easing into the bar may help here. Finally, smile before you begin; this is one that should have examiners tapping their feet!

Schein *arr.* Snell   Allemande   page 4

My trusty but rather ancient *Concise Oxford Dictionary* writes about the Allemande: 'in character it is serious but not heavy and in speed moderate'. That just about sums up this example by Schein – somewhat stately and formal, but with the possibility of some enlivening articulation.

The phrasing in the top part has been carefully marked and observing the shaping in bars 4 & 10, with the smallest break in sound after the third crotchet, will help avoid its being too four square. The accompaniment has been left bare and it is here that some judicious lifting will preserve the Allemande's dance origins. Try making both crotchets in bar 2 articulated, light. Same again for the repeated As in bar 5, and perhaps in bar 4 too. You could use a similar strategy in bars 7 & 8 or you may prefer to keep these bars entirely *legato* as a contrast. This is beautifully crafted with its six-bar halves and use of sequence and repetition. The speed, yes, moderate, but feel that buoyancy in the mood. No need for repeats in the exam.

Reinagle   Minuet (no. 10 from *24 Short and Easy Pieces*)   page 5

Primary triad harmonies, with the occasional ii^b in place of IV, a balanced phrase structure, and a serviceable, if uninspiring, melody. Almost painting by numbers, but still pedagogically useful. The Minuet has three beats in a bar, but really just the one stress, emphasised by also having only one harmony per bar. So it is important to find an unhurried tempo but to feel one beat, one gesture per bar. Later, as Beethoven's Minuets became cheekier and faster, they would turn into Scherzos. The suggested tempo here is excellent; don't let it drag.

Much else is self-explanatory. A little rotary motion, keeping that wrist flexible, will help the LH in bars 5-6 and 13-14. Show us the difference between the two bar *crescendo* in the first of those, and the one bar *crescendo* in bar 14. Only to *mf* though – this Minuet keeps its elegance and does not need anything stronger in dynamic. Is anyone else reminded of another Minuet in bar 9 – perhaps Reinagle paying homage to Bach/Petzold?

Grill   I'm Happy   page 6

There's a lot of moving around the keyboard in this piece, so it will probably suit someone comfortable with the geography of the keyboard. The small phrases and frequent rests cleverly allow plenty of time to move to new positions. Try to encourage pianists to think about where they are going *before* changing position. Distances are usually pretty small, quite often entailing just a change of finger on the same note. Think first, then move – it always reminds me of the 'mirror, signal, manoeuvre' I was taught at driving school!

Some repeated notes come under a slur, as in bar 7 or 11 and, although a real *legato* is not possible, aim to make these long and melodic. Check too that the lower notes in the small chords in bars 15 and 19-20 release and don't linger under the next single notes. The *mp*/*mf* contrast is cleverly enhanced by moving the LH down an octave at bar 9. The double basses have clearly joined in at this point, adding extra sonority, to which the RH must respond. Enjoy the *crescendo* at the end, keeping a good *f* in the bass, down to the bottom C, then cutting everything off with a cheeky *acciaccatura*.

Mower	Just for Starters	page 7

Mike Mower's piece is quite ingenious, and makes me smile every time I play it. There's also something quite sophisticated about the modulations and it reminds me of the way Beethoven can suddenly make a turn into a completely alien key, often as a joke, wrong-footing the listener, but easily finding his way back home.

We begin innocently enough with a C major triad in unison. One bar later and we are in E minor. Back to C, then G. Right, start again. This time we go through F, D minor and Bb. Wonderful! It is important for pianists to understand what is going on, both so that they can enjoy the joke, but also so that they realise they are telling a story as the music twists and turns through these different keys. Which notes are the ones that tell us we are going somewhere new? Those will be the ones to lead towards, to colour, to highlight in some way. No articulation is marked, so you could use that to point up interesting moments, for instance separating the notes in bar 8. Begin bar 9 at a lower dynamic to make the *crescendo* more effective and disappear at the end without the ceremony of a *ritardando*.

Strecke	The Enchanted Garden	page 8

Pedalling is not expected at this level, but we automatically want to see the garden through rose-tinted, hazy spectacles to reproduce that sense of enchantment. Stick as closely as possible to the keys, lightening the second note of the slur, but without releasing it too early. A sigh of wonderment, of suspended belief; we step gently, almost reverentially, through the gate. Release those second crotchets too quickly and the mood will become jaunty and lose its magic. Similarly, the cello needs much subtlety in shaping its fifths from bar 9, supporting the RH melody as you venture further along the path, but not disrupting its *cantabile* character.

The wrist has a large part to play here. It channels the weight of the arm to depress the initial notes, then rises in preparation for the next downbeat, playing the second note of the slur as it does so, making the second note more passive, gentler in sound. Such a useful technique to master and this is a good piece to practise it on. Listen to the pedal D, ensuring there is enough sound on it for us to hear its stability, to hear that our garden visitor is too enchanted to move for 8 bars.

Charlton	Walking (and Talking)	page 9

C major, a relaxed tempo, some repetition and we know how good Kay Charlton is at writing light-hearted pieces. But there is a wealth of detail here, which makes it more interesting than some choices, but demands sharp eyes and ears.

The opening material returns in bar 17 one dynamic level higher. Think added confidence, an extra saxophone added to the ensemble, a brighter colour. Imagination will add extra energy to the fingers, hopefully resulting in the higher dynamic without pushing. A good *p* in the preceding bar will also help the *f* to sound stronger. Notice that the two-note slurs are usually within a *crescendo* (as in bar 4), with the second quaver marked *staccato*, so this is not an occasion for drop-float, instead the second note needs more energy. Strangely the quavers in bar 7 are not marked in the same way, but the effect is almost identical. In bar 2, release the RH minim with the last *staccato* in the LH; to hold it on sounds pedantic. There are several places where both hands have rests, bars 4, 20, etc. Listen to make sure there really is silence and, although it may be tempting, the quavers should be played evenly and not 'swung'.

Gruber   Jodler (Yodeler)   page 10

If you play through this delightful piece, you will easily guess that Jodler means a yodel, or a yodeler. Memories of *The Sound of Music* and the 'Lonely Goatherd' perhaps! The yodels fall beautifully under the fingers, encouraging a gentle rotary motion, but always keeping the fifth finger rounded and supported. If rotary motion becomes too exaggerated you end up using the side, rather than the tip or pad of the finger. Meanwhile the LH has the challenge of putting the weight on the weaker side of the hand, fingers 5 & 4, while making sure the thumb releases with a light touch. Again, check that the LH little finger is not collapsing.

There are basically two lines of music here, each repeated at a lower dynamic, with a *crescendo* in the final bars. This to me suggests the answering call from the opposite mountainside, much further away, so lower in volume. That said, the difference between *mf* and *mp* is not so large, so listen to ensure that *mp* still has substance and that *mf* does not shout! Whether or not you play this as an exam piece, it will be great fun to learn and perform.

Crosland   Hand in Hand   page 11

This twelve- (plus one) bar blues will be popular with examiners, taking very little time to perform at the tempo suggested. Probably also popular with students and teachers – the former because of its easily accessible style, and the latter because of the opportunity it affords to talk about and play around with the 12-bar blues: I, I, I, I, IV, IV, I, I, V, IV, I, I.

Some details worth noting about the bass. The first LH gesture moves forward to the Bb, while the second resolves to the C. Crosland only marks a definite *crescendo* the third time this happens, but it is implicit in the harmonic progressions earlier, just shouldn't be so marked. Another thing to take care over is the length of the final notes of each gesture. I find it very easy to move my concentration to the other hand, and forget that I need to release after one crotchet – so listen out for that throughout the piece. In the RH the release at the end of the first slur will enable the *tenuto*, the slight stress, on the next note. The last chord is not so easy: make a good *rallentando* so that you have time to have all four fingers on the final notes before your arm helps to play them.

Arnold   Across the Plains   *Queen's Temple*

The title suggests distance and space. A crotchet pulse of c. 88 is good, allowing details of phrasing and articulation to be incorporated and registered by the listener. Two things to note: firstly there is a misprint in bar 17; the LH should play in unison with the RH, so its first note should be an E. Secondly there is a long slur over the final four bars; do not mistake this for a tie – the last Bs should be sounded with *piano* accents.

Listen for the fading of the sound on the pauses at the opening. The first two notes are confident, summoning. Then wait until the B has faded to a good *piano*, before the distant echo responds. Again, wait until the atmosphere of the introduction has dispelled before entering firmly with the main theme. Small details, but learning listening skills is essential and this will also create a time-suspended atmosphere. Unslurred crotchets need definition and should not be linked to the next notes (eg from bars 11 to 12 or 14 to 15). The canon effect from bar 7 will need careful practice, and note the stark contrasts in dynamics – playing scales at f or p levels will help, always connecting dynamic to mood: confident vs diffident; certain vs hesitant; bright vs subdued. Perhaps here the effect should be one of near vs far.

Crosland   Can't Stop Myself   *Spartan*

This jazzy piece is based on a twelve-bar blues and shouldn't take too long to learn, with its repetition of motifs and general catchiness. 'Swing the quavers' Crosland instructs. We don't do it as well as the real jazz pianists, but play the quavers as the last of a group of triplets, and that will work very well. Notice the D♯ in bar 9 and the E♭ two bars later. A useful point of theory to talk about there. The accented notes and chords in bars 10 & 12 are not *staccato*, so give these length as well as extra energy. How will you play the sf accented chords in those bars differently from the sf *tenuto* at the end? Maybe the latter has more weight behind the sound, whereas the former use strength to get the accent?

The marked tempo is pretty fast, and something a little less speedy, perhaps around 138, would also be acceptable. No repeat in the exam...and no singing either!

Diabelli   Bagatelle   *Kjos*

Not every young pianist will be ready for the three-note chords in this piece, but it's a reliable choice otherwise, with the simple, classical harmonies that every pianist needs to have under their fingers. No repeats necessary in the exam, and a tempo of around 112 crotchets per minute works well.

The mood is contented rather than jolly and gently separated chords in the bass will help this, while the RH sings its melody *cantabile*. Watch how a supple wrist will naturally adjust as you cover the octave in the opening arpeggio. As soon as you play the second crotchet, the G, the thumb releases the D, and releases any tension too, quickly returning to its usual position beside the second finger. Similarly, once you reach the top D, let the hand find its natural five-finger position, using a 3 to play the B, and then stretching down to the E in the next bar. Do discuss the primary triad harmonies and find the same chords in other keys. I would begin work on the three note chords by playing the outside notes first, watching the thumb change position, then play the top third, using 3 only on the F♯. Pianists should quickly learn these from memory, hearing how each chord fits under the notes of the melody, and noticing how the F♯ is only needed in the chord when the melody doesn't include it in its own part.

Emonts   Tango   *Schott*

That bass line, the first four notes of the descending melodic minor, has been used in countless pieces, yet remains irresistible. It circles around, each time ending on the dominant, so needing to return to the start yet again. The final two bars find a resolution of sorts, although a little abruptly perhaps, but this motif suits the dark, slightly dangerous, twilit world of the tango.

You will want to find a comfortable fingering for the LH thirds – that suggested may not suit all hands. The goal is perfect synchronisation, which means that both fingers want to be resting on the keys before the arm helps to depress them. 1 & 3 are good, but 2 & 4 are ideal as the hand is so well balanced around the middle finger; perhaps try 1/3, 2/4, 1/3, 2/4? The footwork in a tango is often complicated and has to be very precise to avoid kicked shins! One element of that precision needed here is in the rests. Two beats only on the RH note in bar 2; the cutting off of the note, just at the beginning of the third beat, should be obvious in this f dynamic and adds an edge to the mood. A small *diminuendo* in bars 6-8 sounds natural and makes sense of the f in bar 9. The sudden pp is another disturbing moment for the audience. Make it as soft as you can, but always with the melody projecting a little above the accompaniment. The last surprise comes with the final 'olé', as a perfectly controlled drop/float technique helps the final resolution disappear into silence...

Goedicke   Dance   *Trinity*

A strong rhythmic pulse and careful grading of dynamic levels are necessary for a successful performance of this playful dance. Play the *staccato* notes crisply and the quavers evenly, holding the minims for their full value. Ensure that chords are places firmly and listen for all notes sounding together.

This 16-bar piece in E minor has four phrases; the first one repeated three times but with two differences. Notice that the RH in bar 8 is a slightly decorated version of bar 4, and that the last phrase (starting in bar 13) is f (instead of mf). The third phrase (from bar 9) starts p – as you build the *crescendo* see if you can do so gradually rather than all at once.

Graupner   Bourrée   *Breitkopf*

That opening stretch of a minor sixth immediately sets the mood – one that to my mind doesn't quite go with a teddy bear baking a cake for a crocodile! It is one of the most expressive intervals, and the ensuing descent of the line makes the opening hopefulness of the sixth even more touching. This is both stylistically sophisticated and musically satisfying.

A tempo of ♩ = 69 will balance the movement of a dance with the plaintive nature of the melody. The slurs emphasise dissonances and emotive intervals, but also imply that unslurred crotchets should be articulated. No need to play them *staccato*, a small detachment from neighbouring notes is enough, and quavers can be played *legato*. This is typically what we often do in baroque music. The bigger intervals in the bass should also be articulated, for instance in bars 3 & 4. When practising the dynamic contrasts, be sure to do them in both hands, not just the RH. No need for repeats in the exam.

Moss
arr. Wedgwood   The Floral Dance (duet)   *Faber*

This wonderfully cheeky duet, with memories of the inimitable Terry Wogan, begins innocently enough but firstly migrates up a tone, then suddenly changes style as a jazz band takes over the final phrases. Enormous fun, but notice that the melodic material is not all in the primo, so it is useful to teach pianists to sing in the missing bars so that the melody sounds complete.

Some articulation is written in, but that leaves us wondering what to do in other places. For instance, bars 7 & 8: you have to separate the repeated notes, but what about the other crotchets, or the quavers? Well, the answer is that the secondo part plays this material first in the preceding bars, so whatever they do, primo must copy. There's no right answer here, but good chamber music means listening to your partner and responding to what they do. The indication 'more relaxed' and the change to a jazzy style implies using a swung rhythm (as triplets) instead of a tight dotted rhythm as notated. Swing the quaver C in bar 36 too. The notes are relatively simple, but listen to match the sound as the hands pass the themes between them. We shouldn't be able to tell when the right is playing, or when the left, they should blend into one melodic line. Ingenious and great fun to perform.

Rybicki   In the Boat   *Breitkopf*

This is a genuinely touching piece; tinges of F minor add sophistication to the harmonic language, while the melodic material is simple, based largely on one motif, which is inverted in the third line. Very skilfully done and a joy to work on.

Although feeling one in a bar will help create longer lines, it is necessary to express the metronome mark in quavers – around 104 quavers a minute. I'm sure all teachers will encourage pianists to learn the LH as chords to begin with, making sure that they are understood as part of the key, not learnt in isolation. What does the A♭ add to bar 2? If you play an A♮ instead, how does it sound and feel? Why is bar 7 slightly different in the LH from bar 3? Play them the other way round and see how they work with the RH melody. We usually remember what we understand, so discovering the reasons behind what works and what doesn't is important, and will make the next piece using similar harmonies easier to learn. Check that the wrist is free to help find a flowing *cantabile* for the melody and perhaps use the same fingering each time for the same figuration, ie starting on a 4 at the beginning too. One to savour – they don't make so many like this!

Telemann   Minuet   *Kjos*

Telemann deserves a prize for having had a piece in the Grade 1 syllabus for at least the last ten years. This is perhaps not the most imaginative, basically staying with tonic/dominant harmonies throughout, but it has some useful teaching features. Minuets are elegant dances and a tempo of around ♩ = 104 is definitely fast enough when you are manoeuvring around the dance floor in a long, wide skirt. The pulse needs to be stable, unhurried, but buoyant, with a sense of greater lightness on the second and third beats of the bar. Fitting triplets then duplets into the beat will probably not be a problem, but using words is always helpful: 'see how the butterfly lands on the rose' would fit bars 9 & 10 perfectly. Lastly the dynamic contrasts in the second section. Perhaps one group of dancers leads the way, then another smaller, shyer group copies? Perhaps the whole band play the f bars, then a quartet only play the p echoes.

Terzibaschitsch   The First Day at School   *Trinity*

This cheerful piece is not an easy option and you may need some strategies in place to help the LH learn all the chords. One suggestion would be not to worry at first about the actual notes, but to get used to recognising the size of the interval, both by looking at it on the page, and identifying it aurally too. Then practise playing all the intervals – everything from a second to an octave is used here – with the same bottom note, or the same top note, listening carefully to the character of each one and feeling their size under the hand. Can you find a sixth, or an octave, or a fifth without looking at the keyboard? Then, when you have thoroughly prepared the ground, you'll need to learn the specific chords here – four bars at a time, always trying to hear, sing or play the melody on top so that the chords relate to something.

Probably this is one that is better for larger hands; as well as an octave in the bass, the RH also has some wider intervals to negotiate. But it is an excellent opportunity to become comfortable with small chords and to move easily around the keyboard. I would suggest playing the RH generally *legato*, except for the repeated notes of course, allowing a small lift every four bars before the upbeat to the next phrase. ♩ = 120 is a good tempo.

Terzibaschitsch   The Last Waltz (duet)   *Trinity*

A bitter-sweet sadness pervades this attractive and, it must be said, relatively easy choice. The theme is shared between the hands — careful listening should ensure no bumps as they change over, especially on the thumbs — and is heard three times, with only minor adjustments. The test here will be creating a beautiful *cantabile* tone, in *p* at the start, but also in *f* later on. Dynamics should always be relative to mood, and there is no anger or aggression here. The melody moves to the secondo in the middle section and although both parts are marked *mf*, it is the melody we want to hear, so balance the two parts accordingly. Ensemble should be straightforward once everything has started, but playing those first notes together is often a challenge, even for the most experienced. Yes, one person may be leading, but I find that breathing together is always most successful, having that sense of pulse in the body before you begin. There is an interrupted cadence in bars 31–32 to which the primo player should also react.

Terzibaschitsch suggests *con Ped* in the secondo; it's not completely necessary, but if do you use it, make sure the melody is not too blurred, and probably avoid it altogether in the C major section. Discreet pedalling can definitely add to the nostalgic mood, but change frequently. Waltzes should usually feel one-in-a-bar: ♩ = 36 suits this piece.

Trad.
arr. Farrington   English Country Garden   *Boosey*

A memorable tune, collected by Cecil Sharp, and used, we read here, by Morris dancers as one of their Handkerchief Dances. The marked tempo is good; no faster, otherwise it will be difficult to keep the integrity of the dotted rhythm. It needs to be precise to catch the perkiness of the mood. Keep listening to ensure pianists don't slip into an easy-going triplet rhythm.

While the rhythms should be precise, the *staccato* could perhaps be more relaxed. The mood is lively — a sunny Sunday afternoon outing with the children perhaps, and if the *staccato* sounds too crisp, the whole piece takes on a military tinge. As this is an arrangement, dynamics have been left deliberately vague, so this is an opportunity to add some in yourself, keeping its relative folk simplicity in mind. An obvious example would be to play the second line at a different level, and perhaps add either a *diminuendo* or *crescendo* at the very end. Place the final chord with confidence, as the Morris men finish the dance and bow to the audience.

Grade 2

Prószyński   The Marionettes (duet)   page 2

This is enormous fun and at the recommended brisk tempo should be a good party piece as well. There is a long tradition of puppetry in Eastern Europe — think of Martinů's *Loutky* or that the story of *Faust* toured Europe as a puppet play before Christopher Marlowe put it on the London stage. Prószyński has in mind here the mechanical, stiff-jointed movements of the marionettes, reproduced through absolute rhythmic precision, a sharp *staccato* and sudden, dramatic dynamic changes. Perhaps too there is an element of *Punch and Judy* here, with the violent *forte* accents and the *accelerando* as they chase each other off stage at the end?

To get that precise, crisp *staccato* keep the movements small and energised, staying close to the keys. Fingering is as important in *staccato* as in *legato*, but it is easier to change position in the former, so consider whether beginning the RH on 5 is the most reliable option. Sometimes we want to give a fraction of time for *subito* dynamic changes, but that wouldn't be appropriate here. Nevertheless you need to think ahead, preparing in your mind for your fingers to find a different touch, a slower or faster speed of depression. The chords in bars 19 & 23 could be longer, matching the RH. Try ending on 5, perhaps 1, 2, 3, 5, or even using both hands, to give a final kick on the last note.

Fux *arr.* Haas   Almost a Canon   page 4

Johann Joseph Fux was born in 1660 and is probably most well known for setting down in print the rules of counterpoint, rules that are still followed today when students write in strict counterpoint. This small teaching piece has been edited, but the added articulation and dynamic detail is eminently sensible and results in a *scherzando* mood with sudden dynamic changes, crossing parts and a sense of mocking the seriousness of genuine counterpoint.

Listen for the difference between a crotchet that is purposefully *staccato* and a crotchet that gently releases at the end of a slur. They should feel and sound different. The unison D on the last beat of bars 5, 7 and 16 needs a decision: play with RH, LH or both? You want to hear both parts but, especially as both hands would be using thumbs, there is a danger that it could be too loud if played by both. An excellent Kodály exercise to use is to sing one hand while playing the other, developing the ability to genuinely hear two lines at once. I would suggest keeping the bass line *legato* in bars 12-14, and watch out for some sneakily tricky co-ordination at the very end. Finally, this is light-hearted; have in mind a fun occasion and replicate that mood for your audience.

Telemann   Rigaudon   page 5

The Rigaudon is an old French dance, probably from Provençal, and this one captures some of this dance's peasant roots, with its obstinate rhythmic repetitions and straightforward structure. There would probably have been very little musical detail in the original, but the editorial decisions here are good, allowing the hands mostly to synchronise articulation, but with a few exceptions. Perfect for developing independence of the hands and also the ability to listen to two separate lines. Multi-tasking is no problem for pianists...

Telemann was a contemporary of J S Bach and although we may think of the baroque style as being very serious today, the word was originally used to mean something over-decorative or fanciful. Baroque music was often embellished, particularly secular works – just think of all those Handel *da capo* arias that kept the audience enthralled as sopranos and castrati vied with each other to add ever more virtuosic ornamentation. This Rigaudon is not really a piece of that ilk, but you may like to add a three-note mordent on the G♯ in bar 7 in the *da capo*.

Löhlein *arr.* Haas   Balletto   page 6

The main technical challenge here is the thirds, played *staccato* and *legato* in the RH. If thirds are relatively new to you, then this is a good opportunity to tackle them – the demands here are very reasonable and appropriate at this level – but try doing some work on them before learning this piece. Play C major in *staccato* thirds or in slurred pairs, then F major with its B♭ an added hurdle. Listen for perfect synchronisation of the two notes, achieved through having the fingers already on the keys, then using the arm to ensure both play together, keeping the wrist stable, but flexible. There are two fingerings suggested for the same pattern here, in bars 1 and 9. I instinctively began with 2, 1 for the first third, but then moved to 3, 1 for the third quaver, returning to 2, 1 at the beginning of the next bar. So now you have three alternatives to try!

Georg Simon Löhlein was an early classical composer, working in Leipzig for much of his life as a performer and teacher. He wrote important teaching books for both piano and violin, so it is not surprising that this thirds exercise is so well-constructed. The whole piece uses just the two chords of tonic and dominant 7th. Quite ingenious, making the notes easy to learn and throwing all attention on to mastering the thirds and communicating the piece's character. By giving it the title 'Balletto' and having *mf* as the loudest dynamic, Löhlein is asking for elegance, control, gracefulness in execution; the tempo is quite challenging and should be seen as a maximum. Listen for the crotchet rests in the cellos, for the shaping of the two-note slurs, for the different characterisation of the *piano* phrases. A useful exercise in the guise of a piece!

Kukuck   The Rowboat   page 7

This is a rather lazy, almost soulful, trip on a rowboat. It is not essential, but if pianists can reach the pedal then this could be a good piece for pedalling practice, with a change every two beats giving plenty of time to master the technique. Learn to do it quite rhythmically: down before you start, then up/down on the first two quavers of the bar, up/down on quavers 4 & 5 etc. Practise on a scale played with one finger, listening to the notes being linked by the pedal, and have a look at what is happening inside the piano if possible so that you understand how the dampers work. There are places where the pedal is not needed, for instance the last two bars, but generally the effect is good.

Using the pedal will help the sense of gliding on the stream, but it is by no means necessary to play the piece well and would be inappropriate for those who cannot reach the pedals. Instead, hold on to the minim chords for as long as possible before you have to release to repeat the bass note. The melodic line moves into the LH in bar 3, so keep the RH quavers lighter here. We say that sometimes when Schubert moves into the major the effect is to deepen the sadness, invoking bitter-sweet memories of a happiness that will not return. There's something of this in the final bars as our trip comes to an end and we return to dry soil.

Moore   The Ballerina   page 8

The ballerina depicted here sounds rather young and inexperienced, eliciting an 'aah' from all who watch. She loses balance for a moment in bar 10, gains confidence for her biggest leap yet in bar 16, then shyly runs off stage at the end. The challenge will be to keep the delicacy and sweetness in this; the tempo is moderate and the bass sets the mood with gentle *pizzicato* quavers. As always, fingers stay close to, if not on, the keys, and see the picture, imagine the sound you want before you begin.

The RH semiquavers want to be beautifully even and smooth, a graceful arm movement before the gentle foot taps on the quavers. Small wrist movements will help the slurs in bars 4 & 5, and the whole arm should be involved in the accent in bar 10. Keep the pattern of smooth semiquavers, short quavers in bar 15, and imagine this picture of increasing self-belief for the *f* here, finding a sound that is confident, rather than strident. You may like to do some re-arranging in the tricky last *pp* bars, perhaps taking the RH F and E into the LH to make the melody easier to control, or the last middle C into the RH to give the LH more time to prepare the *acciaccatura*. Understated, subtle and rather lovely.

R Mohrs   Shepherd's Melody   page 9

Both hands remain in a G position throughout, but this clever piece contrasts a rather doleful *Largo* section with a dancing central *Allegro*. Minor becomes major; bare open fifths turn into harmonic major thirds; the tempo more than doubles. Find a story behind the transformation: something happens to change the lonely shepherd's mood – a passing circus? watching a family of rabbits chase each other through the field? Whatever it is disappears, and he returns to his melancholy...

This is another piece where some discreet pedalling would help to link the drone chords, just as the breath through bagpipes also helps to make the sound continuous. But the piece works perfectly well without. Remember to make the *forte/piano* contrast in both hands in bars 11–13, relating the dynamic levels to the mood, not allowing the *forte* to shout. You may like to move the LH to play the thirds in the middle section with 2 & 4, a better balanced hand perhaps, changing back to a G position for bar 23. Allegro is a tempo marking but also implies liveliness, and here there should be no pedal, and the unslurred quavers will sound more light-hearted if articulated. No repeat, but the *da capo* is essential.

Cleaver   Persian Holiday   page 10

The bass motif makes me think of camels, their humps swinging from side to side, and the augmented 2nds in the melody are of course shorthand for the East. Both these elements are immediately appealing but don't be fooled, this is a tricky little piece, full of articulation detail that demands complete independence of the hands. An excellent workout for the brain.

Find a comfortable swing within the hand to achieve the bass slurs. This is something of a caricature, so you can enjoy the drop-float effect, always ensuring that the fifth finger does not play on its side. We often forget that the thumb also moves independently – playing it with the whole hand will make it heavy, and here you need to avoid that. Once the physical movements of the LH are engrained, it will be easier to maintain the integrity of the melody's articulation on top of the camel's lurching gait. Begin bar 15 softer than the dynamic you've reached to make the *crescendo* effective and keep the *ff* in the context of an energetic holiday excursion – fun, not fierce!

V Mohrs   Poor Mouse   page 11

The story here is crystal clear, the only question is whether the chord at the end is the cat getting the mouse, or the mouse finally escaping...perhaps the title provides the answer!

The *acciaccaturas*, crushed notes, help emphasise the accents. We would expect the one in bar 2 to be D♯ to E, so approaching the E from above is an inventive surprise. Experiment with fingering – I found 3, 2 in RH and 3, 4 in LH easier to synchronise. There are two places, bar 12, LH, and bar 16, both hands, where we have crotchets that are neither *staccato* nor slurred, so hold these for their full length. Each line has a *crescendo* (the mouse trying to leave its hole?), dropping back again at the beginning of the following line, with the final *crescendo* taking you all the way to the *ff* climax. It's not easy to start *pp* on a piano you don't know, but you need to take a risk, barely pressing to the bottom of the key. Have that pulse ticking away in your head before you start – perhaps sing the first line through to yourself to find the tempo and character. Keep to the suggested brisk speed; the mouse is justifiably jittery, the cat poised to pounce. Just one note of caution: the aim is to excite your audience, not necessarily to get excited yourself. A warm heart and cool head will help you communicate the mood, but stay technically in control.

Crosland   Bendin' the Rules   *Ferrum*

This is a rather simple piece at this level, so examiners will be looking for all the musical details to be fully incorporated into the performance. Two in a bar with a variety of articulations: a sharp, cheeky *staccato*, edgy accents, weighted and slinky slurs. Some of the last are two-note slurs with lightly released second crotchets, but some end on a *staccato*, implying a more active, strongly played last note. Bars 13- 15 have the same music as the opening, but suggest a different arrangement of the hands. It may be worth experimenting with using this at the beginning, as long as the RH knows exactly where to find its chord in bar 3.

Once all the detail is in place, the mood should look after itself. Jaunty, swaggering, confident. Note though that there is nothing aggressive about the piece; the main dynamic is *mf*, which gives room for the accents to make their mark without having to shout. An extra thrust from the arms should help with the *sfz* at the end. At ♩ = 76 the whole piece should take precisely one minute. Perfect!

Gurlitt   Peasant Dance (duet)   Breitkopf

This duet gives the RH a good workout. Firm, well-supported fingers staying close to the keys and played with plenty of energy from the bridge of the hand will find the *f* at speed that is requested. Avoid making the arm heavy; remember that the note needs to be depressed *quickly* to sound *forte*, and you want to feel the release in each finger as soon as it has played. No pressing down with the arm or hand. The frequent *staccatos* are useful, places where you can check that the wrist is completely free. Listen for rhythmic evenness in the semiquavers and adjust the fingering if you need to. It's good to practise bar 4 using fingers 5 & 4, but in performance you may find 3 & 2 more dependable. At the *p* imagine that one of the dancers has a solo, then all the others join in again as the opening music returns in bar 13. ♩ = 92, and observe the *scherzando* – this needs to sound as though the performer is having fun, so get an appropriate picture in your head before you start.

Haydn   German Dance   *Kjos*

Haydn was undoubtedly one of the great classical composers, in many ways making possible the often more lauded developments of Beethoven. But they all had to start somewhere and they used to practise writing small pieces to harmonic formulas; I suspect this is one such. An opening fanfare delineates the bright D major triad, a more elegant reply deploys a small sequence, then cadences in D. The following four bars unceremoniously take us to A major, the elegant theme returns and all is over in under a minute at ♩ = 126. No repeats in the exam.

Formulaic to some extent, but are there traces of Haydn's future eminence? I enjoy the contrast between the stronger sections that have three equal beats in a bar and what I've labelled above as the elegant reply, which favours the first beat, eschewing any chord on beat three, and sounding momentarily more like a graceful Minuet. As well as listening for the difference in stress between these sections, you may like to add a little dynamic variation to highlight the characters of each line. There is something satisfying about it – perfectly balanced and with a nod to a more French elegance that softens its opening directness.

Knipper   A Cavalry Song of the Steppes   *Breitkopf*

Lev Knipper studied with Reinhold Glière, another composer often favoured by examination boards, and fought in the Russian civil war. This cavalry song is melancholy, bleak and heavy-hearted, but also rather haunting with its use of the flattened seventh and primary triads in root position. The Russian steppes are vast grasslands and the weariness entailed in crossing them is manifest in these dark, stern bass chords. A crotchet beat of 104 captures the determined, but weary mood.

It is worth trying different fingerings on the triad. 1, 3, 5 may suit many, but 1, 2, 4 is also an option. I like to use the latter on the C minor chord, then the former as the hand goes down to G minor in bar 4 – it makes the two chords seem more connected. Perfect synchronisation of all three notes may take some practice. Try just playing the open fifth first, making sure the hand is well-balanced, then add in the third, usually a black note, making sure to have all three fingers resting on the notes before you play them. It's also important that the chords allow the melodic material to be in the spotlight. Keep them separated, but all the same length, no pedal, and no more than *mf* (probably *mp* from bar 11). Use plenty of arm weight to make a full, vibrant sound for the melody, keeping it *legato* above the chords. Have a picture in your mind before you start – see those soldiers in their ushankas on horseback looking out over the steppes...

| Lvov-Kompaneets | The Sparrow | *Trinity* |

This descriptive piece in C major relies on a lightness of touch and spirit for its effect. Pay careful attention to the articulation markings, making sure to phrase off the slurred groups delicately, and to give emphasis to the *tenuto* crotchets (bar 4, 20, etc).

The piece is in ternary (ABA) form, the B section (bars 9–16) in the dominant key of G major and marked *forte*. The composer has an interesting surprise for us when the A section returns. Several unexpected flats appear in the last phrase, outlining the chord of Db major (in the key of C major this chord is known as the Neapolitan 6th). What effect does this have on the mood, for you?

| Lysenko | Raindrops | *Breitkopf* |

These raindrops have not kept you inside, rather you seem to be out there among them, running around and thoroughly enjoying the experience. Even the forays into A minor remain cheerful and the final *sf* is positively triumphant. A crotchet pulse of 76 is good.

Melodic movement is mostly by step and fits extremely well under the hands. The *staccato* wants to be very light and crisp to recreate the rain, but that doesn't mean lifting high off the keys. Staying close to the keys is always safer, more economical, and usually makes a more precise sound. Keep the wrist supple to help shape the small slurs and use the arms to give extra thrust for the last chord. You can make up exercises away from the keyboard to help the hands achieve independence of articulation; games like playing a scale *legato* in one hand while singing *staccato*, and vice versa, are also fun to try. I would also get pianists to imagine a story behind the music. Why C major in places and A minor in others? Why *p* here and *mf* there? What happens at the end? This will help cement the dynamics in their minds and bring the whole piece to life.

| Menken | A Whole New World (from Walt Disney's *Aladdin*) | *Faber* |

'I can show you the world / Shining, shimmering splendid / Tell me, princess, now when did / You last let your heart decide!' sings Aladdin as he and the princess fly on his magic carpet. You can watch the clip from the film on YouTube; Aladdin is rather free with his rhythms and the tempo is quite fast. For the purposes of the exam, ♩ = 96 moves without hurrying, allowing plenty of time to find the chords; just the second repeat; and the rhythms should be played as notated!

Pedal is indicated just at the end, but be sure to check the pedals before you start. Some pianos have three, and all of us have pressed the wrong one by mistake at some point! The chord playing here is quite sophisticated, and it is never too early to get ingrained some good practice. For instance, substituting fingers: the suggested fingering in RH bar 18 is not ideal, completely breaking the melodic connection between the C and G. My preferred option would be to substitute a 2 for the thumb on the F on beat 2, then play the third chord with 3/1. Not essential, but a useful technique. Knowing and loving the tune will make many want to choose this, but it isn't an easy option by any means...

Strecke — Rustic Dance — *Breitkopf*

There are several imaginative pieces by Kerstin Strecke in the syllabus. She was trained both as a pianist and artist and now works as both in Frankfurt.

The harmonies here are simply tonic and dominant, justifying the 'rustic' tag. But the key is A major, so a little further away from C than usual, and a good key to explore, with longer fingers fitting neatly on to the black notes in chords and scales. I would suggest learning the tune without the chords, swapping between hands as necessary – it's so good to have the LH share the spotlight. Then see if you can work out which chord fits under each bar just by listening: is that a comfortable tonic bar, or is it a bar with more tension, needing the dominant 7th under it? Hear the two chords as tension and resolution, shaping the phrases accordingly – this is the basis for so much music and beyond. No repeats in the exam please, and a tempo around ♩ = 120.

Terzibaschitsch — The Little Locomotive — *Trinity*

What a clever idea this is, to have the train accelerate out of one station, chug away to the next, and then gradually apply the brakes. Probably not the first time it's been done, but effective nonetheless. The main body of the piece can go at a locomotive speed, around 192 chugs (crotchets) per minute. This is another piece that uses just two chords, tonic and dominant 7th, so spend some time feeling confident about them, playing them in all inversions, as arpeggios, broken chords, etc. Then you are off: just two positions in the LH to find and, as I suggested elsewhere (see Strecke above), see if pianists can hear which chord it should be under the RH melody, rather than just read it. They should learn to identify the bars that move away from home, from the tonic, and improvising on these chords may also be useful to develop this aural skill.

Be sure to get both hands involved in the whistle blasts – maybe the ensuing p is because someone has covered their ears? The *accelerando* at the beginning always seems much easier than the *ritardando* at the end. To help the latter, keep hearing the LH crotchets in your head through those rests, getting slower and slower...and stop.

Terzibaschitsch — The Gondola (duet) — *Trinity*

Based almost entirely on two gently rocking harmonies, this is quite a hypnotic duet, and the secondo is repetitive enough to perhaps enable a friend to be involved, preferably one who can add in the pedal as well. Marked 'sad', this is not the usual serenade on a gondola, but perhaps a trip made alone, remembering a time when you were with friends. Hear the LH taking over the melody in bar 7 and passing it back to the RH in bar 8. Both hands will play the same phrase in unison a few bars later and this is a tricky moment for the LH, involving either a big stretch (you could start on 5 and stretch to the thumb for the higher E) or crossing over up a fifth. If you choose the latter, as is indicated in the score, then remember that the pedal is managing the *legato* for you and it is legal to let go in order to make the movement smooth and avoid raising the elbow. The addition of the pp notes in bars 23 & 25 is a nice touch from Terzibaschitsch, and will require a sensitive touch from pianists, light fingers, barely pressing to the bottom of the keys. Synchronise the last chord by breathing together. Keen-eyed pianists will spot the missing tie in the LH in bar 18.

Wedgwood   Pterodactyl Take-off!   *Faber*

The drawing of a rather nervous dinosaur at the bottom of the page is most definitely not a pterodactyl but this popular book starring prehistoric animals is useful to have for pianists going through the obligatory dinosaur phase. A jazz waltz is one that leaves out the third beat in the accompaniment – think Satie's *Gymnopédies* – giving a more relaxed mood to the whole.

There are some ambiguities in the marked articulation. Does the slur in bars 3-4 imply non-*legato* in bars 1 & 2? My suggestion would be to see the slurs as riding on the thermals, swooping and ultra *legato*, whereas elsewhere perhaps you're needing to flap those enormous wings to stay up there, so find more buoyancy in the *legato*. Meanwhile that descending semitone bass line in the rather beautiful B minor middle section – ah, it works every time doesn't it? – suggests to me that you could detach the bass notes in the first section, throwing a little more emphasis on to the chord, whose top note shadows the melody. Schubert often uses accents where he wants an emotional stress, and I think that is the case in bar 18. You don't want to hit the top A, but realise its expressiveness against the bass A♯ and colour accordingly. Wedgwood's tempo and words of advice are excellent as always.

Grade 3

Schmitz   Tango-Prelude II (duet)   page 2

The composer has marked the articulation of almost every single note in this piece, leaving no room for doubt over his demands. The exceptions are the upbeat Gs in bars 8 & 10, which will inevitably be *staccato* at this tempo. The piece is also in unison until the very end – quite an easy option at this level, although having to play that first section four times may deter some…

Notice that the final beats of bars 9 & 13 are *tenuto*, matching the *legato* in the secondo part. Generally *staccato* crotchets and *staccato* quavers can be the same length, but those with accents need extra energy to make the note descend faster. The rhythms need to be absolutely precise – there is a great deal of fancy footwork in the tango, and one missed semiquaver and one of the dancers will have a sore foot! A note to the secondo player: your bass line is a great counterfoil to the top part, but you'll probably want to keep those chords well under the marked *forte* level so that they don't intrude too much into the texture. The bracketed notes should not be played by you, as the primo player needs them. The concertina or bandoneon is a popular choice for tangos, and having that sound in mind for the secondo chords will help.

Couperin *arr.* Snell   Le Petit Rien   page 4

François Couperin was primarily a great composer, but also wrote one of the most important treatises for performers of baroque keyboard works, *L'art de toucher le clavecin*, published in 1716. One of his aims was to merge elements of French and Italian styles, and in *Le Petit Rien* there is a simplicity and sunniness, which could well evoke thoughts of Italy.

'The little nothing' – something akin to a bagatelle perhaps, light-hearted and to be thrown off in performance as 'twere a mere trifle. To achieve that ease of course takes many hours of both planning and practice. It is written in two parts, so play one and sing the other, making sure that both parts are equally shapely, that the bass line is not a mere passenger. Work out the natural phrasing, following the implications of the harmonies: bars 3 & 4 answer bars 1 & 2, but are in the dominant, slightly more intense and, similarly, bars 7 & 8 answer bars 5 & 6, but are lower, finding resolution. This constant play of tension and relaxation goes beyond the areas of dynamic marked on the score, but will bring the whole to life, keeping it alive and interesting, as though invented on the spot. Musical detail here is probably editorial, but wisely chosen. Keep a sense of buoyancy in the *staccatos*, no tension in the wrists; *staccatos* do not want to sound overly clipped, but rather fit with the general easy-going character of this delightful 'nothing'.

Scarlatti   Sonata in G major   page 5

Domenico Scarlatti was employed at the Portuguese court to teach the princess Maria Barbara the harpsichord and some of his 550 plus sonatas were written for this purpose. When the first set was published, he penned a preface to say that the sonatas aimed to delight and entertain both performer and audience. Domenico was born in the same year as J S Bach and Handel, whose goals I would suggest were not always the same. Nonetheless, 1685 was definitely a vintage year.

Scarlatti often delighted and entertained through virtuosity, through display and exuberance, hand crossings, repeated notes, arpeggios traversing the whole keyboard…it is all there in his sonatas. But there are also many that are deeply expressive and lyrical. This example falls in the middle: the RH does have some more acrobatic moments but the tempo is *andante*, emphasising lyricism and giving pianists time to concentrate on sound and shaping. Given the steady pace, repeats should not be played, although generally I would urge performers to preserve the balance of the condensed sonata structure in Scarlatti and never to play just the first repeat.

Find a difference in articulation and character between bars 1–6 and the more *scherzando* bar 7, returning to lyricism in bars 8–9, then again more animated in bars 10–11. Some discreet pedalling may help, changing every quaver, contrasting with a poised, pert *staccato*, resisting the temptation to speed up on the *staccato* quavers. To match the more lyrical mood both arpeggios in bars 5–6 will want to be played *diminuendo*, avoiding bumping the last note as you think about moving the hand down for the next arpeggio – you have plenty of time, as long as you know where you are going. A sophisticated choice.

Graham   Between the Fingers   page 6

Peter Graham has written a very effective piece, immediately attractive and relatively straightforward note-wise. It is also an exercise in pedalling, although there is some ambiguity in the markings – discussed below – and a useful way of practising two-against-three divisions of the beat. It has a gentle fluidity – feel one-in-a-bar – but it is also very lyrical. The interpolated quavers in the bass shouldn't take away from the singing top part, and there's a moment in bars 9–10 when the top E needs to be heard for three beats, finally resolving on the D. A touch of *rubato* occasionally, perhaps to highlight the harmony in bar 11, or the climax in bar 23 would suit the mood, and the comma in bar 27 implies a complete lifting of the sound before the final pleading cadence.

It begins with one pedal per bar. Open the piano before you begin, ie depress the sustaining pedal, then quickly but quietly lift then depress it on the first note of each bar (no need to do it for bar 1 of course). At ♩ = 100, you could make the pedalling quite rhythmical, lifting and depressing in the rhythm of two quavers. This pedalling should be used again from bar 13. Once you are comfortable with the principles of *legato* pedalling, understanding what is actually going on inside the piano to make it work, then I see no reason not to use it throughout the piece. Instead of lifting the pedal completely for the third beat of bar 9, I would suggest changing it, and changing again for bar 10. It is ultimately much easier to keep pedalling than to stop for the odd beat and, more importantly, it is less likely that you will blur harmonies, as can often happen when you put the pedal *down* at the beginning of the bar, rather than changing it, up *then* down. Pedal with your ears – if the RH notes are part of a chord, pedal through, if not, then change. So bar 25 will probably need a change per crotchet. Every pianist needs to develop good pedalling, which sits alongside good listening skills, and this is a perfect piece to practise on.

Schönmehl	Rain	page 7

This is a gentle, sweet offering from Mike Schönmehl, who has written many accessible pieces in an easy-listening style. Decisions to be made over articulation and one tricky technique to master, but otherwise straightforward and very relaxing both to perform and to listen to. This rain shower is brief, fades during the last line and surely the sun emerges with the last chords?

Given the subject matter, play the chords *staccato*, with a gentle wrist action – not too crisp, just the mild patter of a shower. The RH will also play non-*legato* at first, making it easy to involve the arm on the thirds, helping synchronisation. Small gaps only in between the notes, maintaining the integrity of their relative lengths. From bar 9 the sustained lower C encourages you to play almost *legato* in the top line until the two *staccatos* in bar 12 lead to the hands swapping roles. The tricky moment comes in bar 7, with the two thirds marked *legato*. To achieve this you need to release the lower G in the first chord so that it can be re-struck as the top note in the second chord, keeping the top part smooth, even though the lower part isn't. A good technique to master that will later become indispensable. As the shower disappears enjoy the *ritardando* and *diminuendo*, perhaps using the pedal for the last two chords, controlling the arpeggiation so that every note is crystal clear as the sun comes out.

Bullard	Model T	page 8

This is the Bullards in jazzy mode, but do look up Alan Bullard's arrangement of *Hushabye Mountain*, in the alternative list, for another example of their work. The Model T was an early make of an American Ford, revolutionary in that it was more generally affordable. Very dashing and the sort of car you may see on the London to Brighton veteran car run today.

Attention needed for musical detail here. Notice that the last two notes in the RH of bar 2 are not slurred, so should be separated. Note too that the D has an accent, but not the F. Similarly in the main motif it is the second crotchet in the middle of the bar that has the accent. Make sure you are doing something physically different to differentiate these – extra energy in the fingers, or help from the arm for the accent. Bars 12 & 14 in the bass change dynamic with phrasing detail mid-bar. Practise by releasing and *stopping* after the first slur and feeling the difference in your fingers and hand as you prepare to play the next note at a different dynamic. Repeat, making the stop shorter and shorter until you are playing in time. To capture that 'jaunty' mood, keep the rhythms precise, listening for exact timing of the rests, keep the *piano* playing cheeky and the dynamic never louder than 'fun' until the two honks on the car horn in bar 23.

Donkin	Badlands	page 9

I predict this will be a popular choice and is indeed great fun to play. Perhaps it is the title, but it brings to mind easy-going cop shows, where the crimes are non-violent and the baddie is always caught at the end. Those were the days...

Christine Donkin has meticulously marked how every note should be played. So, no excuse for not being equally meticulous in your observance of all the detail. The minims, as in bars 2, 6, etc, should release as you play the fifth quaver in the bass, bridging the gap between the fourth *staccato* quaver and the semiquavers. At this brisk tempo the semiquavers will need careful practising, and consider different fingerings. You could use 1, 2, 3, 4 for those in bar 2, and 2, 1, 2, 3 for those in bar 6 for instance. Practise relevant scales at this speed and think about making the finger movements economical and precise. The whole piece has attitude; dynamics are *mf* and *f* (be sure to have a different instrumentation or character in mind to colour these) and slurs end with a *staccato*, with definition and not a passive release. Finally, relish the bars where the bass line emerges into the spotlight. Very cleverly written – enjoy!

| Crosland | The Clown and the Ballerina | page 10 |

A fun concept, imaginatively written, and featuring Neapolitan harmonies that will be good to improvise around. The dynamic landscape is various levels of *piano* for the ballerina, with something stronger matching the complete change of mood in bar 9 for the clown.

Feel the lean on a well-rounded fifth finger for the bass F, while the top part of the hand is loose and light for the thirds. Find colours to identify with dynamics: a shy flautist for the *pp*, a friendly clarinettist for *p* and a confident oboist for the *mp*. It will be important to have that brighter oboe sound in bar 29, to make the following *diminuendo* possible. You can have fun with the circus clown music; Crosland marks 'clumsily' and I would interpret this by the smallest of rhythmic distortions, very slightly elongating the first beats to emphasise the rougher, uneven movements of this character. In contrast the ballerina is all elegance and a carefully calibrated *ritardando* will bring her graceful twirling to a close. Have fingers on the keys for the final chord, then very gently push the keys away from you.

| Rollin | Sunrise on the Matterhorn | page 12 |

This is atmospheric and immensely appealing as well as being pedagogically sound. *Legato* pedalling throughout with the heel on the ground and the foot always in contact with the pedal to be as quiet as possible. Rollin begins with a sunrise motif: a rising D major arpeggio, shared between the hands and marked to develop from *mp* to *mf*. This is quite a subtle *crescendo*, which will almost happen by virtue of the sustaining pedal, the build-up of sound and the increasing brightness as you go up the keyboard, so take care not to overdo it, listening to make the joins between the hands seamless. It is good to remember that the arm is responsible for putting the hand in the right place, so feel the arm doing its work as the LH moves back down the keyboard to play the chords in bars 3-4. Check that the shoulders stay relaxed – there's often a temptation to raise them as we move along the keyboard. Enjoy the sound of the flattened median chord in bar 3 – unusual and perfectly chosen here.

The contrasting B minor melody is accompanied by an Alberti bass. Practise this as chords, checking for a balanced hand with a good bridge, then keep this shape as you play as written. The accompaniment wants to sound a dynamic level lower than the melody, but within that the bass note of each broken chord is most important, so allow a slight lean on fourth and fifth fingers. A good *cantabile* touch is required for the melody, so get the arm involved. The harmonies used are unusual, but worth discussing and perhaps improvising around. If the progressions are understood, they will be remembered and hopefully easily found even under pressure. Perhaps you haven't watched the sun rise over the Matterhorn, but remember your response at seeing something equally beautiful and touching before you begin, so that you convey this mood to the audience.

Arens   Praeludium vocis mollis a   *Breitkopf*

This piece is from *Piano Misterioso*, a collection of 28 pieces by Barbara Arens. It is relatively easy to play – all white keys, all fitting beautifully under the hand and with the tried and tested descending melodic minor motif in the bass. What's more, you can watch the composer herself perform it on YouTube.

Pedal is essential here, so only for those of you who can comfortably reach it, keeping your heel on the ground. The foot should keep in touch with the pedal at all times to avoid any extraneous noise and basically it lifts with each new bass note, releasing the sound of the previous bar, then depresses again to catch the new harmony. This works very well in the second half when the RH plays towards the top of the keyboard and you can probably hold the pedal for four bars at a time between bars 17 & 24. But at the beginning the melody is in the middle of the keyboard, playing consecutive notes, so you may wish to delay depressing the pedal, or change it again within the bar, so that the melody doesn't become too blurred. This is a sophisticated technique and demands concentrated listening, but it is worth developing. As with all performance art, we need to be alive to what is happening in the moment; the piano, the room, our heartbeat – all will probably be different on the day of a performance, and we need to stay aware and respond accordingly. This is what makes performance so exciting and endlessly interesting.

J S Bach   Polonaise in G minor   *Bärenreiter*

A master at work – this is perfectly constructed and both dignified and touching. Interestingly there are two other Polonaises in the *Anna Magdalena Notebook*, both in G minor, so maybe a key Bach associated with this dance. Of the two Polish dances that Chopin would later transform through his patriotism, the Polonaise is the more stately, with its main stress safely grounded on the first beat, rather than springing on to the second as in the Mazurka. A tempo of ♩ = 80 is good here, and I suggest that playing the first repeat balances the whole, and gives the opportunity for a change of dynamic.

The wedges in bars 11 & 13 are original, but otherwise you are free to decide on musical detail. Nothing too complex – this has a serious air and dynamics should relate to the musical structure. The modulation to B♭ major, the return to G minor, and the repetition of material are probably events that could be dynamically highlighted. As a general guideline next door notes, small intervals and faster moving material are all more likely to be *legato*, whereas larger intervals and broken chords would often be articulated, for instance bar 3 & 4 in the bass, or the octaves in the RH. There is nobility and poise in its characterisation; be sure to keep the dotted rhythms precise and beware of hurrying those separated crotchets in bars 11 & 13. If you enjoy this, do look for the other two – both seldom heard.

Elgar *arr.* Bullard   Chanson de matin (duet)   *OUP*

As the note at the bottom of the page helpfully tells us, Elgar originally wrote this for violin and piano, with the violin very much in the role of soloist, so the challenge here is to produce a singing melody in a variety of dynamics, with exquisite phrasing and a gentle expression. No small task! On the other hand, except for a few bars, the primo part is in unison, with a rich B minor (think cello concerto) solo in the middle of the piece. Experiment with balance, perhaps, for instance, letting the lower octave project more in the *da capo* for a darker timbre. Get the arm involved in the *sonore* section, helping to make that rich, noble sound we associate with Elgar.

The articulation no doubt follows the bowing in the solo violin version and should be carefully studied, noticing differences such as the lighter first beat in bar 17 or the new bow in bar 19 compared to the longer phrase in bar 3. Ultimately though accompaniment and solo are being played on one instrument, and the pedal that the secondo player will instinctively want to use may hide some of this articulation detail. The answer is for the secondo to be aware of the top part's phrasing, but also for the primo player to show the articulation through shaping the sound as well as releasing notes. Secondo players: the terraced dynamics from bar 9 onwards are really up to you to engineer through your down beats. Listen to good YouTube performances and try to reproduce the fluidity and flexibility of the violin sound. There is a delicate freshness here, but also a melancholy, a nostalgia, which needs to project. ♩ = 80 is good for capturing both. The notes are fairly easy, but there is much musical subtlety here.

Kelly   Almost a Waltz   *Spartan*

Bryan Kelly is teasing us, wrong-footing the performer in at least three ways, with his rhythm, harmony and articulation. In turn we need to relish the piece's idiosyncrasies and aim to make our audience smile in disbelief as well as in pleasure. Perhaps the cheekiest thing of all is the quiet, unexpected exit. Oh, and I'm sure there's a misprint in bar 20: the third crotchet in the RH should be a G.

A tempo of 152 crotchets per minute may seem fast but of course waltzes are generally one in a bar, making the crotchet pulse relatively fast. Five beats per bar, with the main accent on the first beat and a weaker stress on beat four. This changes in bars 11 & 12, where Kelly achieves the effect of a hemiola, moving the stress so that instead of dividing the bar into 3+2, the main accent shifts in bar 11 and bar 12 becomes 2+3. Wonderful. Enjoy the 'wrongness' of the accents, but with a smile − *forte*, not ferocious. The main challenge though is the articulation of the LH, which goes counter to what one expects in a waltz, with the *tenuto* chords, and also against what the RH is doing. You need to find a length in the articulation while hearing a small separation between all the crotchets. Perhaps an obstinate tuba player who will only play his notes one dynamic and one length? Using the arm to find this articulation will help.

The *crescendo* in bar 13 is oddly placed. It makes sense to underline the alien key of A major − how did we get there? − and the highest note at the beginning of bar 14. But to continue the *crescendo* beyond there is counter-intuitive, which is probably part of the game Kelly is playing with us. Try your best, but avoid forcing the sound. The important thing is to bow out with the least of fuss, leaving your audience gasping at your audacity.

Kelly   Spanish Dance   *Trinity*

A tempo of ♩ = 100 is appropriate at this level, rather than 112 as marked. It is very easy to feel the spinning movement in the quaver patterns of this colourful and descriptive piece. Your task as performer is to bring out the humour in the music. Bar 5 is an extra bar tacked onto the first phrase, and the effect is as though the dancers have lost their footing. The rests in the phrase beginning in bar 10 certainly give a feeling of hesitation, and the way the final cadence is interrupted (from bar 42) suggests giddiness from too much spinning.

Rhythmic precision and accuracy are required here, and the accents need to be very clear and incisive. Hold the pedal through the last 2 bars, and enjoy the final flourish. The last chord is not A minor as we might expect, but something much more exotic.

Kodály   Children's Dances No. 2   *Boosey*

I remember when I was taught about learning styles that the example used was: when you get a new gadget, do you immediately turn it on and start using it, do you read the instruction manual first, or do you try to take it apart to see how it works? I suspect few of us do the second nowadays but in this case it is essential. There is a line at the top of the Kodály in paler ink telling us that this should be played on the black keys...

It is constantly surprising to find how many young pianists avoid using the thumb or fifth finger on the black notes. Yes, sometimes there is a better solution, but quite often it is a useful way of keeping the hand balanced and the only main adjustment we need to make is to move into the keyboard. Some composers use the black keys for their pentatonic associations, and keys like Db major or Bb minor may also have more lyrical associations. In these cases it can be useful to use the pad of the finger, a slightly flatter, fatter touch, which works particularly well on the narrower black keys.

Although there is a melody here, the character is that of a dance, with the main theme firstly played shyly in the RH, and then reiterated firmly by the LH. Notice the phrasing in bars 5-8; think of the tonguing of a wind instrument, or the intrusion of a strong consonant into a vocal line. Listen for the held minims in bars 8 & 10, feeling a leaning on one part of the hand while the upper fingers feel loose and active. Choose a tempo of around ♩ = 100.

Mier   Dance of the Gypsies   *Alfred*

The first four notes of the descending melodic minor scale are summoned here as a symbol of the gypsy soul. Yes, very much a cliché, but this is an effective piece in the hands of an imaginative pianist, with a brief cadenza in which one of the gypsies whirls around in her flared skirt...

Claps and foot stamps introduce the dance at a brisk tempo of dotted minim = 63. Use the arm to help those LH accents, an inward and upward thrust through flexible wrists into the keys to release them with energy. Keep the pulse ticking over in your head to keep track of the molto *rit.* through the tied note in bar 9, gradually cranking up the excitement again into *Tempo primo*. Instinctively we want to *crescendo* with an *accelerando*, so to do the opposite here will need practice – try it on some scales as well. Have a picture in your head for the cadenza: perhaps the whirling starts slowly and gets gradually faster into bar 34, or the dancer may begin spinning very fast and gradually run out of steam? You can choose fingering to suit your picture, for instance a turn fingering, 1, 4, 3, 2, 1, may be better for a quick start. Pedal is essential in the two places marked and could be used elsewhere as well. This needs to be performed with character and flair; these gypsies relish their independence and outdoor life.

Schumann   Wilder Reiter (The Wild Horseman)   *Wiener UT*

Schumann's wife Clara tells us that Robert decided to write his own children's pieces because he found so few pieces of quality for his daughter, Marie, when she was learning to play. He originally wanted them published with illustrations, although this proved to be prohibitively expensive, but one edition reproduces an engraving of a young child on a rocking horse at the top of *Wilder Reiter*, and it is that picture of a wild rider that we should have in mind, and nothing more fierce.

Schumann's *Advice to Young Musicians* is full of wonderful exhortations and a couple that apply here are: 'Play strictly in time! The playing of many a virtuoso resembles the walk of an intoxicated person' and 'Do not think velocity...your highest aim. Try to produce such an impression with a piece of music as was intended by the composer.' (from the Henle edition, 2007, 75-77). Looking closely at the music to see what the composer did intend, we see that the main dynamic is *mf*, indicating that this is fun, not fierce. Interestingly the *sf* in the outer sections is marked in both hands, but in the central F major section it is in LH alone. This will help the theme in the bass to maintain its dominance and not be drowned by over-enthusiastic RH chords. Take some time to analyse and improvise around the chords; if they are well understood, they will be remembered and easily found. All those dots are liable to produce high hand gestures – resist! Keep close to the keys for precise, accurate playing. Perform at around dotted ♩ = 88 and no need for the repeat in the exam.

Sherman & Sherman
arr. Bullard   Hushabye Mountain (from *Chitty Chitty Bang Bang*)   *Faber*

This is an absolute gem. Originally sung by Dick Van Dyke as inventor Caractacus Potts in *Chitty Chitty Bang Bang*, it is beautifully arranged here by Alan Bullard, each version of the melody differently orchestrated. Play with a crotchet pulse of c. 88 and ideally with some discreet pedalling.

The melody requires a warm, *cantabile* touch, the arm involved to help the notes descend in a slow, controlled manner to the bottom of the keys. The phrases are long – try singing them: 'A gentle breeze from Hushabye Mountain / Softly blows o'er Lullaby Bay'. Notice how you need to keep sustaining through 'gen-' on the minim to finish the word, 'gentle'. Of course, on the piano the notes start to decay immediately, but listen through the long notes, playing them firmly enough to last through the tie, then balancing the sound of the quaver so that it does not bump within the phrase. This is what playing *legato cantabile* is all about. Hear the melody in your head, preferably sung, or on a melodic instrument like the oboe, and then listen to the sound as you play, coming as close to your ideal as you can.

When the melody is repeated you have sustained notes in the bass, a line of descending semitones that often tugs at the heartstrings! This is where some pedal will help to blur the broken chords to create one harmony, rather than separate notes, while the melody in the RH needs enough weight to project above this. More of the orchestra enter in bar 18, then gradually phase out until barely anyone is left playing at the end and the children are asleep. 'Wave goodbye to the cares of the day' whispers Caractacus.

Tanner   Cheesed off in Amsterdam   *Spartan*

A fun title for a fun piece. What's more, as in Donkin's *Badlands* (see above), every note is carefully marked with a *staccato*, an accent or a slur, so there is no ambiguity and no excuse for not playing it exactly as written! The recommended tempo is brisk, but good.

Mark Tanner is a multi-talented pianist, writer and composer and perhaps also being a performer has persuaded him to annotate his scores so meticulously. No ambiguity here. Keep those dotted rhythms exact – your annoyance results in an edginess, manifest in the *staccatos*, accents and the tightly controlled rhythms. An easy, triplet swing would be inappropriate here. You'll need to be rigorous about the rests towards the end too. Using a metronome is good once or twice, but you need to feel the pulse in your body, perhaps filling the rests by hearing in your head an echo of some of the music you've just played. The rests shouldn't be an *absence*, but a real presence, an amount of time where pressure either builds or dissipates. Note that Tanner cleverly orders '*faintly*' disgruntled; with much of the piece played *forte* and numerous accents, you need to guard against forcing the tone. Save something for the final *ff* but at the end the audience should laugh, not cower.

Terzibaschitsch   The Little Elf   *Trinity*

This is perhaps one for a younger student, albeit one who can reach the pedals easily, keeping the heel on the ground. John Thompson sacked his elves some while ago now, but as a symbol for sweetness and innocence they match this music well. Feel one beat in a bar, but at a tempo of around 132 crotchets per minute.

Terzibaschitsch marks *staccato* on the crotchets in the first section and I expect she intends us to play the quavers *legato*, always contrasting with the *staccato* fifth in the bass. Remember when you begin that you need to leave room for the even softer dynamic in bar 9 and, to control the low dynamic levels, stay close to the keys, making your movements small, with the wrist free to cushion the small push from the arm for the chords. Technically the *crescendos* will happen if we press the notes gradually more quickly, but creating a narrative, perhaps plucking up the courage to push those reeds apart to look around, then hiding again, is often better at achieving the result you want with younger pianists. *Legato* pedalling is asked for in the middle section – practise this with the LH alone at first – and notice the longer pedal for bars 24-28, releasing it only at the end of the pause (not at the beginning of bar 28 as the pedal mark itself seems to indicate). Of course the first section plays with the 'blue moon' harmonies, so could be a useful starting point for some improvisation sessions. Musically very straightforward, but not without charm.

Grades 4-5

At Grades 4-5, candidates will typically be able to support their intentions in performance by demonstrating a sound understanding of material, leading to a more personal and imaginative interpretation, in which there is a reasonably consistent application of developing technical skills. Performances will be clear and well-projected with appropriate volume, control of pace (including variations in speed), control of tone quality and appropriate application of instrumental colour (eg tone control) to support mood and character. Candidates will show evidence of sensitivity to and considerable control of material. Effective preparation and study will lead to a secure, accurate and sustained performance which will engage the audience. These features will be demonstrated through material which is substantial enough to convey some development, in terms of both the composer's intentions and the candidate's interpretation. Content will be sufficiently complex to provide some internal contrast and range (eg the preparation and achievement of climax, or a ternary form movement with a contrasting middle section). There will be a stylistic variety of musical language and form. Some subtleties of syntax will provide opportunity for a variety of approaches and interpretative choices (eg choice of articulation patterns in a movement from a baroque suite).

Grade 4

Kirnberger   Minuet in E major   page 3

What an unusual term 'festivo' is, conjuring up thoughts of holidays and festivities, which suits the character of this cheerful minuet very well. The suggested tempo is challenging, given all the articulation detail to negotiate, but appropriate, and particularly necessary as repeats are requested for the exam. Kirnberger was one of J S Bach's students and a composer more known for his academic writing, both in musical style and in his theoretical studies, but there is little sign of that academicism here. Instead we have a celebration of E major and its related keys, with motifs formed from fragments of scales and broken chords.

A good starting point will be to visit these keys, practising scales and arpeggios in E, A and B majors. Try playing with different articulations too, perhaps four notes slurred at a time, or five slurred and one *staccato* (as in bar 5). We need to examine the score with a toothcomb: there are several quavers at the ends of bars that need separate articulation; many places where the hands play different articulations; and check the penultimate bar, as the pattern changes and is likely to catch pianists out. Crotchets that are unmarked are up to you – probably separated, but not as short as those with *staccato* dots. The energy and joy must not be lost in *p*; keep the fingers active. There's a saying for singers, sing softly but speak loudly, and you want something like that here – a stage whisper perhaps. With the many black notes in this key, there are moments of tricky fingering. What is suggested is generally good, but remember it is not illegal to use a thumb on a black note. For instance, I would play both the A and G♯ either side of the barline, bars 5-6, with a thumb, maintaining a good hand position for the ensuing quavers. Lastly Kirnberger has been fairly even-handed with his distribution of melodic material, so give the LH its fair share of the limelight.

Mozart   Allegretto (from *The London Sketchbook*, K. 15hh)   page 4

Wolfgang Amadeus wrote this when he was eight years old. He and his sister Nannerl were in London with their father and it is thought that the collection of pieces known as *The London Sketchbook* were composed while Leopold had a serious throat infection and the children were forbidden from playing the piano and disturbing their father. The pieces were written in pencil (very blunt and difficult to decipher in some cases) and contain the odd mistake or inconsistency. Here we see that the RH F in bar 16 is a dotted crotchet, merely a crotchet in bar 46, but a dotted crotchet again in bar 62. Should they really be different? I doubt very much that Mozart would have minded either way, but a little variety is seldom a bad thing.

The LH semiquavers in the D minor section will need careful practice to flow confidently. I'm not fond of using dotted rhythms as they tend to develop jerky movements, but you could instead try stopping every 4 notes, changing the note you start on, making sure those four notes are smooth and comfortable under the hand. I also like working backwards: play the last two semiquavers in bar 28, ending on the G in bar 29. Then add the previous two notes, then the whole of bar 28, then from the last two in bar 27, etc. You can also play it literally backwards, which really checks that you know the fingering and precisely where the hand has to be.

Bar 30 is a conundrum: was this a mistake of Mozart's, asking the RH to hold the D, whilst restriking it with the LH, or was he perhaps imagining an instrument with two keyboards? Either way, we need to find a solution and I suggest restriking it with the RH and then holding it as the LH plays the rest of the descending scale. Other solutions are possible!

No pedal is required; it wasn't in general use until much later than this. There are decisions to make about dynamic. For instance in bars 17-24 you will probably alternate between highlighting the RH for two bars, then the answering LH, and of course with so many repetitions of the main theme it would be entirely appropriate to vary the tone, perhaps finding a lighter colour for the reprise after the D minor section. The unedited Urtext is a gift for experimenting with aspects of articulation and dynamic, matching both to mood and character, developing your imagination and technique along the way. Here decisions about articulation have been made for you, but it is good to know that they are editorial – the original pencil score has no such markings.

Mozart was of course a child prodigy and it is apt that this *London Sketchbook* found its way, probably through Mozart's wife, to another child prodigy, Felix Mendelssohn, whose family later gave it to a library in Berlin.

Burgmüller   **Barcarolle, op. 100 no. 22**   page 6

The gondola is tethered to a post, gently rocking in the water. First one, then another tourist steps in; the gondolier casts off, and serenades the couple as they sail down the Grand Canal in Venice.

Small adjusting wrist movements with fingers close to the keys will help to achieve the *legato* and *diminuendo* for the rocking gondola in the first two bars. Wait for the boat to steady itself after those first three chords – try to avoid counting the pause, instead listening to the sound and judging when is the precise right moment to re-start the *pianissimo* rocking. The second pause, moving to an unexpected C major, will be even longer, the *crescendo* more intense, with the LH *acciaccatura* adding impact to the climax without interfering rhythmically with the melodic progression from C to E♮ in the top voice. The chords will benefit from being pedalled, and some pedalling in the following *dolce* bars will help the couple get comfortable on their cushions. The serenade itself is probably accompanied by guitar or lute and if you do add some pedal to soften the edges of the chords, keep it discreet and be sure to separate them from each other, giving space in the texture for the serenade to project easily.

This barcarolle comes from a book of studies and it is the singing of the main melody that is being practised here, keeping the LH supportive, but in the background. Your fingering should be comfortable, allowing the weight of the arm to be carried from note to note. Check that wrists are flexible and above all listen to the sound, imagining it carrying gently over the water. A real *staccato* in bars 28 & 29 (does the boat bump the side of the canal here?), but keep the *sforzando* within the subdued dynamic. The penultimate *lusingando*, 'coaxing', phrase brings us back to the bank and as the gondolier ties his boat back to the post, perhaps he discovers, *perdendosi*, that the couple have fallen asleep. A beautifully structured piece, attractive, imaginative and pedagogically sound.

Elgar   **Andantino (1st movt from *Sonatina*)**   page 8

This is the first movement of a two-movement sonatina written for Elgar's niece. Tender, wistful, almost hesitant in places, yet also full of Elgarian warmth and generosity. There are several performances on YouTube, and the one by John Ogden is particularly beautiful, if a little slower than advised here.

It is difficult to *teach* the sense of style needed for such a piece – the *rubato*, the handling of the *largamentes*, allowing the music space to speak. I recommend listening to other works by Elgar, the *Enigma Variations*, the cello concerto, maybe the *Sea Pictures* or some of the symphonies. He has come to represent something quintessentially English, which is often linked to both reticence and nobility, but Elgar is also a masterly orchestrator. All of those elements are here: notice how the orchestration is different at the return of the theme in bar 25, with added *pizzicatos* and a sustained note in the horn; there is hesitation in the small phrases in bars 33-36, a gathering of confidence before the heartfelt *largamente* melody finally finds the courage to sing with certainty. Pedal throughout will add depth to the sound, being careful though not to sustain through rests, and both analyse and hear where the *appoggiaturas* occur and shape accordingly. Bar 6, bar 10, bar 12...listen for the difference in meaning between the two notes as tension turns into resolution, as the sound diminishes and the bar relaxes. The LH fifth finger has an important role, sustaining some of the bass notes, playing them with slightly more weight than the other accompanying notes. The *acciaccatura* in bar 23 is short, but lyrical, heightening the expression in the *allargando*. No repeat in the exam.

Gedike   Little Piece no. 17 (from *20 Little Pieces for Beginners*)   page 10

Yes, Gedike is simply a variant spelling of Goedicke. Alexander Fyodorovich Goedicke was a Russian composer, first cousin to the more celebrated Nicolai Medtner. Examination boards keep Goedicke's name alive, but he is little heard in concert halls. Nevertheless pieces such as this are well-crafted and contain a wealth of musical detail in the service of a dramatic narrative, making them pedagogically useful as well.

The title is not helpful and I would encourage students to imagine their own storyline to match the colourful music. Someone runs on stage, stops, looks around searching for someone else...you get the picture! Articulation needs to match the character of the music: the *staccato* at the opening will be crisp, urgent, whereas in the *con anima* something less spiky will go better with the minor key and more pleading character. The upbeat to bar 32 should probably be the same as the other upbeats in this section, non-*legato*, making the reiteration of the F♯ in the LH possible, although a touch of pedal would not go amiss here. Small slurs abound and will need consideration. Some, as in bar 4, show the resolution of dissonances and need shaping with dynamics. Some build the tension, as in the opening gesture, or the scale in bars 15-16 (which should surely end in a climactic *staccato* in both hands). Others, as in the *Tranquillo*, seem to be marks of bowing, with slightly stronger down bows on the first note but with no major gap between up bow and down bow. Lastly, consider the silences as areas where things happen – tension dissipates or a new idea comes to the character – they should not feel empty. A good moment to talk about pregnant pauses perhaps? As Gedike instructs, be confident, be bold, and tell a story as you perform this.

Gardel
arr. Farrington   Por una Cabeza   page 12

This is the first of two tangos in this selection, based on an original song for which Carlos Gardel wrote the music, Alfredo Le Pera the words. *Por una Cabeza* refers to a horse winning a race 'by a head' and the words talk of the singer's love for gambling and women...perhaps one not to research too closely! In both the sung versions and the arrangements for violin that abound on the internet there are many *portamenti* and many distortions of the rhythm. But for exam purposes keep the rhythms in the first section precise, not allowing the dotted rhythms to sag, but perhaps allow a little more leeway in the chorus, the A minor, with broad triplets more pleadingly lyrical above the tango bass.

Everyone has their own method for teaching two against three, as we have on the second page here. Nice cuppa tea is a firm favourite, and understanding the maths behind the combination, actually drawing the beat divided into the common denominator six, the second quaver fitting in between the second and third triplets, helps some learning styles enormously. Before playing the notes here, practise the rhythms on something much easier. Remember to use the arm to help with the thirds, a small impulse ensuring good synchronisation. Then add the foot into the mix...and of course, the character – this is quite rich and impassioned. A tricky few bars! In the first section use the wrist to help shape the RH phrases, small adjusting movements negotiating the black notes and ensuring that the fifth and sixth semiquavers taper effectively. There's a real tension between the upright exactness of the LH and the more shapely, weaving RH. In a way this represents an aspect of the dance, with the man generally leading, whilst his partner often has the more fancy footwork. Not an easy choice, but very satisfying when played well.

Badings   Ballo gaio   page 15

Coming in at around 30 seconds, this will give examiners little time to write, so be prepared to wait before your next piece! Dynamics are f or p, with one *crescendo*. During that *crescendo* the first notes of the bars are marked with accents, so listen for those increasing in volume as well. The p is both times accompanied by *leggiero*, so use a lighter touch, a gentler *staccato* than in the f sections, where the sound wants to be firm and direct. Imagine finger tips made of different materials – a crisp, starched linen for the f and a softer silk for the p. The *marcato* in bar 6 seems to relate to the LH, encouraging you to bring it more into focus for its solo motif, and notice that there is no *crescendo* at the end. Stay *piano*, if anything fading as you climb up the keyboard, with that very disconcerting overlapping of hands and phrases. The final chords, which are not marked *staccato*, are a final wink to the audience – despite the quasi-pompous opening, the whole thing has really been a piece of fun, a merry dance.

Henk, or Hendrik, Badings was a largely self-taught Dutch composer, who died relatively recently in 1987. Despite writing many large scale orchestral works, probably most of us have only come across his compositions on the exam syllabuses. A shame – there is wit and craft in this miniature.

Moore   Waltz Mystique   page 16

This mystical waltz has a fetching, rather forlorn theme that fits well under the fingers and should be quickly learnt. The harmonies are well chosen; the descending semitone bass is undoubtedly a cliché, but it nevertheless works well, and the foray into the Neapolitan major on the second page is particularly memorable. The challenge is in the variable articulation of the waltz accompaniment, changing from the first bar, whose slur throws the stress on to the second beat of the bar, to bar 5, where a sustained bass rings below detached second and third beat chords, to bar 10, which is neither one nor the other.

The central section moves into major territory and the dynamic comes up from the opening p to a more richly coloured mf. A good response to this change of mood would be to add in some pedalling, avoiding blurring the melody, but enabling the accompanying chords to sustain and add warmth and support. The rests in bar 27 signify a link back to the opening material, and this would be a good place to play *senza ped.* again as we approach the return of E minor. The *ritardando* in bar 30 will help ease back into the recapitulation. Experiment with playing the thirds in the first four bars divided between the hands and in bars 37-39 you could try playing thirds in the LH, leaving the RH able to project the top line more easily as you fade to pp. Do observe the short repeat in performance.

Arens   Tango Passionis   page 17

Barbara Arens has a piece in Grade 3 as well and once again it is possible to watch a YouTube clip of the composer herself performing this passionate tango. However, she does not stick exactly to the version published here, with some added sixths in places and some pedalling over rests. There is a long debate to be had over being meticulously faithful to the score or faithful to the spirit of score, and you could argue that listening to a composer's performance is evidence every bit as strong as the score itself. However, the score will be the primary source material for examiners and my advice would be to play what is written there rather than what you hear on YouTube.

Arens asks us to pedal with discretion. Use the pedal to enrich the sound, and to join what would otherwise be unjoinable, particularly the repeated sixths in bars 13, 17 & 19. Keep the integrity of the LH *staccato* as it occurs in bar 2; that is what gives this tango its straight-backed poise. As in Gardel's tango above, there is a subtle contrast between the more flexible, lyrical top part, and the firmness and rigour of the rhythmic interjections. Keep the LH close to the keys – jumping too high for the *staccatos* will make them sound looser, which is not what you are listening for here. More instruments seem to join in from bar 9; use the arm to find a full, deep sound on the sixths. The unusual *ritardando* then *accelerando* leads to a *forte* repeat of the opening. Take care not to shout here, easily done as you return to the middle of the keyboard. Instead make an effective *crescendo* and end with elan, *fortissimo*.

C P E Bach   Andante   *Faber*

This exquisite miniature by J S Bach's most well-known son is a real test of intimate, expressive playing and would have been well-suited to the gentler forebear of the piano, the clavichord. C P E Bach is associated with the *Empfindsamer Stil*, a style of writing that was more personal, more sensitive than that of the baroque period, and the poignant harmonies, wide-ranging, chromatic top line and the gentle comments from inner voices all add to the tender mood depicted here.

Many details to work on. Mordents should be on the beat in this period. One rule tells us that if a trill is preceded by the upper note, then it should begin on the note. But here I would suggest beginning both trills on the D. The previous D finishes a phrase and starting on the upper note adds dissonance and extra expressivity, as well as making the trill of demisemiquavers perfectly even. Bach asks for pedalling, but take care that this is used primarily to join the chords and not to blur the melody, which wants to be heard as from a solo instrument. Avoid holding the pedal for a whole minim, but rather listen to the integrity of the top line and change, or delay depressing, as necessary.

There are several places when the LH divides into two parts, bars 3-4, 5-7, etc. Practise these lines with two hands to hear the sustained notes and also to check which notes need to project more, to comment on or duet with the melody, then be sure to keep listening once you put it back together as written, checking that you can hear all three lines. Intervals do not all cost the same; a minor sixth should be more expensive, more expressive, than a major third. Hear the beauty of the diminished 7th in bar 9 and shape accordingly. The minor sixth in bar 15 seems a last reach towards an answer that never comes; give these special moments room to impact on a listener. Similarly the *tenuto* marks in bars 13 & 14 are to stress the chromaticism, just as you might lean on 'pain' when saying 'painful'. Not for everyone, but a joy for those awake to what it has to offer.

Bertini   Study in E minor   *Trinity*

This is a study in rhythmic evenness and finger control of fast triplet patterns, which both hands are required to execute with equal skill. The tempo is lively and the mood turbulent.

Make sure both hands sound precisely together at the beginning and end of the slurred triplet groups (ie bars 1-2), and taper the phrase off so we hear a very clear *diminuendo*. Crotchets not under a phrase mark should be detached (assume a *staccato* touch). The slurs in bars 8 and 16 apply to the triplets only; the crotchet above will be short. Pay careful attention to the part writing in the RH in bars 11-12; insist that long notes are held and shorter notes released. Avoid a *crescendo* through bar 14 – the *ff* at bar 15 needs to be sudden and dramatic.

Grieg Walt in A minor *Schott*

Edvard Grieg composed groups of *Lyric Pieces* throughout his life, the first when he was in his twenties and the last set six years before his death. The beautiful Arietta, the very first one, has been a Grade 5 piece and is now in Trinity's *Raise the Bar* volume. Grieg memorably revisited the same melody in his very last lyric piece, Remembrances, thereby coming full circle, reworking the material in the light of a further 34 years' experience. This Waltz is the second in the first set, directly following the Arietta, sharing some of its quiet melancholy.

Grieg directs performers to use the pedal but, whereas the first section has a plethora of *staccato* dots, the slurs in the central A major section suggest a more lyrical, *legato* approach. Even the accompanying chords here are marked *portamento*. So my advice would be to use the pedal on the first beat only for most of the A minor section, but to use it far more generously in the A major. There is a problem with the contrasts between *staccato* and *legato* in the two hands on some downbeats, for instance bar 5. My solution is to play the top note of the first chord with the RH, allowing the LH to make the *legato* between bass and chord without the pedal. Easy once you get used to it. The A major part also has its challenges. Some nifty fingerwork is needed in bar 39, the RH releasing the C♯ so that the LH can play it, and then vice versa – another reason for the pedal being essential here. The *acciaccatura* is also surprisingly tricky: it should come before the beat in this romantic style, so you are effectively repeating the G♯, but making it softer the second time so that the stress is on the downbeat dissonance, the F♯. You may like to try swapping the hands for this section – it works surprisingly well! Keep the *f* in proportion to the overall mood, and maybe use *una corda* for the final *pianissimo* bars. Much repetition here, so it is nowhere near as long as it looks, and a tempo of around ♩ = 138, with a definite sense of one-in-a-bar works well.

Kirchner Dreaming Lake *Breitkopf*

What an unusual piece. Over before you know it and packed with detail. Discreet pedalling enhances the sound world; you will probably want to change with most quavers, adding a slight aura of mistiness around the edges of this lake. A tempo of ♩ = 58 is good, but keep this flexible – there is no metronome ticking as your raft floats on this dreaming lake.

Theodor Kirchner led a chequered life, but was well-respected by his fellow German romantic composers, such as the Schumanns and Mendelssohn. He wrote many such miniatures, some of which find their way on to examination syllabuses, but they are often, as here, musically sophisticated and need sensitivity and subtlety in performance. The slurs in *Dreaming Lake* should be seen as phrase marks – a gap in the sound is not appropriate. The handovers, as one instrument after another plays the rocking motif, should be unhurried and respond to the harmonies. The second voice takes us up to D minor – heightened expressivity here – then the next two voices bring us back to A minor and down an octave, so shape those accordingly. Even where no dynamics are marked this piece is continually in flux, moving up and down on gentle ripples of sound. Careful voicing needed in the next exchange as a smaller motif works its way down to the middle voice in bars 7-8, making a *ritardando* en route, and with a sustained bass line bringing things to a half close. The *crescendo* in bar 14 needs to be enough to take the tension through the rests, but not to be too shrill on the top octaves. The *staccato* should also fit the story, separated, yes, but not too short to disturb the sleepy atmosphere. By giving us a descriptive title Kirchner has given us licence to build our own narrative – what's your story?

Maxwell Davies   Calm Water (from *Stevie's Ferry to Hoy*)   *Boosey*

This is a piece to meditate by; you can't play it well if half your mind is thinking about something else. It demands complete focus, a sense of being in the zone, of switching off from the world's hassles and losing yourself in the moment, in the peace of this music. Three minutes of mindfulness! So much of Peter Maxwell Davies' music was inspired by the special atmosphere of the Orkney Islands; he is already much missed.

As the ferry takes you back to the Orkneys the waves gently overlap each other, the RH needing to hear two individual voices rather than chords. When the melody enters in the bass the sound can be a little fuller. Notice how the phrases again overlap, with a singing five bars in the cello, playing with a different moment in the top parts' cycle as it repeats – listen to be sure your phrasing captures this subtlety. The pedal can be used discreetly throughout the piece, but time seems to stop with the Bb – so far we've heard only white notes – and the pedal here is held over 7 bars. I hear the Bbs as bells, a warning that the ferry is approaching land through the mist. Give them extra depth and ringing projection. This music is reworked on its return, and notice the long pedal from bar 47 to the end. The hands are crossed here, but then uncross as the RH plays above the LH, the last line marked two octaves higher, and barely audible. Check posture when the LH crosses over – no need to raise the shoulder! *Calm Water* needs a calm pianist with care for sound and mood. Around ♩ = 108.

Mozart   Menuetto and Trio (from *Viennese Sonatina no. 6*)   *Universal*

This is a challenging choice for Grade 4, with a lot of material to learn, alongside copious musical detail. It also requires a sophisticated understanding of this refined Mozartian style, and it's long, so no repeats in the exam and be ready for the examiner to stop you before the DC. In my edition the metronome mark is 72 to a bar, but this is too ambitious, and a crotchet pulse of 132 is more realistic for this level, keeping more or less the same tempo for the trio. An important consideration is that these are arrangements, not original Mozart. He wrote them as wind divertimentos in 1783 and we are not sure who arranged them – probably Ferdinand Kauer, but definitely not Mozart. There are places where the articulation is awkward and counter-intuitive, for instance in bars 3 and 41-42. It is based on the wind parts, where individual instruments can more easily play contrasting articulation, but definitely in bars 41-42 I would suggest you separate the LH sixths to match the RH.

Do listen to the original version, K439b. The emphasis is on gracefulness, precision, elegant shaping of all the phrases, and an avoidance of any harshness in the *forte* playing. Listen for the shaping of 6/4 to 5/3 progressions as in bar 4 – such a staple element of this style. The dynamic contrasts in the trio should be achieved through increased use of arm weight, but always keeping the wrist supple, able to transfer the weight into the keys without unnecessary tension. There is a fun bassoon solo in bars 37-40 in the trio, so allow this bass line to project while the oboe weaves a quaver line above it. I doubt whether anyone would have danced to this divertimento, but there is still that buoyancy in the pulse, a poise in the rhythms that you can often find by imagining conducting a group, the physical gestures, and the looking towards different instrumentalists helping you to inhabit the pulse. Ultimately the whole piece needs to sound effortless – the most difficult challenge of all. But I do hope that some pianists will be courageous enough to take it on...

Neefe Arioso *Bärenreiter*

This rather lovely Arioso also sounds like an arrangement, perhaps from a string trio this time. Christian Gottlob Neefe was a contemporary of Mozart's and was primarily known for his operas. But he was also one of Beethoven's early teachers and there is something about the richness of the writing that reminds me of the sort of theme Beethoven may write and then use as the basis of variations. As the title suggests, this is mainly a solo aria for the first violin, with occasional interpolations from the other players, and demands a singing tone, careful balancing of all three voices, and good foot control.

The opening cello gesture is noteworthy and needs shaping, a *diminuendo* as you relax down the octave. The majority of the footwork is *legato* pedalling but you could use direct pedalling for bar 17, for variety and to respect the *portamento* articulation. Direct pedalling means that the pedal is released and depressed as you release and depress the notes, rather than the opposite, giving you a small space between the chords. There are other places with similar markings in the RH, but with *legato* in the LH and I feel it sounds pedantic to highlight the difference in this context, so would use the *portamento* indication as a reason to lift the RH, ensuring good synchronisation of the sixth, while maintaining *legato* pedalling. Listen carefully in bar 19 – you may want to delay depressing the pedal so as not to blur the syncopated violins. The middle section features more of a duet between the top two voices. Keep the dotted rhythms poised and precise and consider playing the second violin with the LH in bar 14. You could slightly ease the tempo into the recapitulation. Throughout feel those top fingers tingling with the special vibrato that the solo violin will use to project this simple but noble theme. The thumb should feel looser, holding on to its longer notes, but allowing the first violin's line to be bathed in a warm, mellow spotlight.

Petot You Have to Shake It *Kjos*

I'm sure that this will appeal to many although put beside the Mozart, Neefe, Maxwell Davies, etc, there is relatively little musical interpretation required! Nevertheless, there is a time-honoured tradition of having a blues in the Grade 4 syllabus and Petot has given us a particularly energetic example. Originally the blues grew from an oral tradition, with a vocal line improvised over the primary triads, with the 12-bar blues developing into a sequence of I, I, I, I, IV, IV, I, I, IV, V, I, I. The mood was, as the name suggests, usually melancholy. Petot has taken the harmonic structure, but made the mood more upbeat, eschewed melodic content, given 'funky' as a direction, and written a particularly creative coda.

Start by improvising your own blues to become fully comfortable with the chord structure. Try using Petot's substitute for the subdominant in bar 9 – a wonderful supertonic with both major and minor thirds. This F♯ is part of the blues scale on C, as are the B♭s and E♭s, so work those into your improvised melodies. The actual notes of this piece should then be quickly learnt. Notice the *loco* in bar 25 and don't automatically make a *diminuendo* with the *ritardando* at the end – it's not marked and it fits the mood more to stay *forte*. Try not to be too pedantic about the triplets – they need to sound easy and insouciant. The repeated chords in bar 12 need to lead back to the opening, so begin them a little softer so that you can *crescendo* into the next downbeat. Make sure your arm is behind all the thirds, staying close to the keys and with little fingers well supported from the bridge. Examiners will be well aware that this is an easy choice, so listen out for every detail, keeping that high-octane energy, albeit controlled from a cool head, from the first to the last note.

Sutermeister   Erster Ferienmorgen   *Schott*

The first morning of the holidays – definitely a cause for celebration, which is just the mood Sutermeister has captured in this piece. As so often with two-page pieces, there is quite a bit of repetition and most of the semiquaver work is scalic, so should lie quite comfortably under the fingers. It would be worth revising Bb major before starting.

The *staccatos* want to be quite chirpy, with extra energy in those marked with an accent. Watch out for the odd chord marked with a line instead of a dot; these want to be held for their full length. Neat part-playing needed in bars 7-8, checking that there is a four-note D major chord sounding on the last beat. For the central section the hands swap roles, the theme passing into the LH. One of the most difficult things to do is to play such five-finger patterns well, particularly when the *crescendo* is towards the fifth finger. Although the most obvious fingering is to use 1, 2, 3, 4, 5 on consecutive notes, if this is not working well then 1, 2, 3, 1, 2 is a possible alternative – or even 1, 2, 3, 1, 4. The contrasting dynamics will help bring the last lines to life. The $\boldsymbol{pp}$ marking does not just mean very soft, but is also full of anticipation; the $\boldsymbol{ff}$ is exultant, not hard. Notice the change from G to Gb in RH, bars 19-20 – easily missed! A fairly straightforward piece, painted in clear, bright colours. Performers need to be able to project this sense of excitement, without getting too excited themselves.

Terzibaschitsch   The Old Gramophone   *Trinity*

Vinyl is making a comeback, so maybe younger pianists will have experience of the needle getting stuck. If not, the joke behind this will take some explaining but it is cleverly done.

The needle gets stuck three times. When it does in real life there is an ugly sound as it catches, then it takes a second to re-find the groove. Terzibaschitsch has written a $\boldsymbol{sf}$ on what is clearly in context a wrong chord, and lets us choose how many times the needle catches before it sets itself to rights. I suggest that you slightly fall forward (rhythmically!) into the $\boldsymbol{sf}$ then take a fraction longer than usual to find the next note. To anyone who has experienced it, this slight distortion of the rhythm comes naturally but for the young and innocent there is no doubt somewhere online where you can hear this happening! Try not to have the same number of repeats each time – it's probably better to decide how many to do, but some of you may wish to be inspired in the moment.

Apart from this imaginative trick, the rest of the piece is also delightful, with a typical, detached waltz accompaniment and a lilting melody. It is the very contrast of the elegance of the music and the ugly distortions that make this such fun, so employ your most graceful phrasing elsewhere, and check that you don't physically tense when the needle is sticking. 56 bars a minute, and as fast as you can safely manage the coda.

Trad. *arr.* Holt   Bop Goes the Weasel   *Spartan*

A clever play on words for this entertaining and ultimately fairly straightforward piece. All the directions you need are written into the music and the suggested tempo is excellent. Dotted rhythms to be swung, played as easy-going triplets, and that includes places, like bars 4 or 26, where you have a combination of dotted crotchet and quaver. *Acciaccaturas* should be played crushed just before the beat. Note that where there is no slur notes should be articulated, so *legato* for the first half of bar 8, then non-*legato* thereafter. Bars 13-15 are the most devious: first you have a quick change from *legato* to non-*legato* in the RH, working against the longer LH chords, then the RH has *staccato* crotchets against those marked *tenuto* in the LH. Well, this is Grade 4, so there need to be some challenging moments! It goes without saying that if you cannot stretch the octave, and easily play the *acciaccatura* in the final bar, then this one isn't for you. The mood is jaunty, swaggering, hands in pockets, so make a full sound for the $\boldsymbol{f}$ passages – hear those trombones joining in – but keep the smile in the sound.

Grade 5

Haydn   Andante in A, Hob I:53/I   page 2

This is an arrangement Haydn made of the second movement of his Symphony no. 53 in D major, Hob 1:53, with the nickname of *L'Impériale*. It is considerably shortened, and there are many other differences, but it is useful to hear a good recording – one using period instruments perhaps – to get a sense of its elegance and lightness. The original has crotchets in the accompaniment rather than quavers, but they are not fully sustained, so support the melody's buoyancy. Most of the upbeats are dotted rhythms, whereas in this arrangement Haydn only throws them in occasionally, and you can hear the strings slurring the first semiquavers in bars 17, 19, etc, to acknowledge the *appoggiatura*, then slightly detaching the last two – very difficult to achieve on the piano without its sounding too pedantic!

With that moving, grazioso tempo and the warmth of the string sound in mind, we can now look at the piano score. Haydn sent a set of ten pieces to be published under the title *Différentes petites pièces faciles et agréables pour Clavecin ou Piano Forte*, almost all of which were arrangements of orchestral movements. Quite how much trouble he took over them is debatable, given the inconsistencies, but there is no doubting the agreeableness of this one. Avoid the pedal in the first A major section, perhaps touching it briefly to highlight the unusual turn of events in bar 9. You want a gently detached articulation that steers a middle ground between a clipped *staccato* and *legato*. Then all change for the A minor. Remember that pedal was not used as frequently in this period (around 1786) as in, say, middle period Beethoven but, used discreetly, it may be appropriate here to change the quality of the sound, being sure to return to detached articulation for the cadential quavers.

Haydn begins the variations shortly after the opening returns and you could use the crotchet vs. quaver LH chords as a prompt for changing mood and dynamic. So bars 41-42 could be *piano* and *legato*, then a more energetic approach to the next two bars with a jump to the syncopation in the RH and firmly separated quavers in the bass. Keep that energy for the next two bars, then finish more smoothly as the chords revert to being crotchets. Unfortunately Haydn doesn't maintain this in the next section, but you can still play with musical detail to reflect the changing harmonies. One constant throughout is the slurs at the ends of phrases, stressing then resolving dissonances; these are a vital ingredient to produce the classical elegance in such pieces. Practise using the wrist to help control and soften the release, using weight on the first chord and just sounding the second as the wrist raises. Once you've mastered that technique, you will use it countless times in the future.

Camidge   Scherzando (from *Sonata no. 1 in G major*)   page 6

There is nowhere to hide in this classical sonata movement. Matthew Camidge came from a family of musicians and was a contemporary of Mozart's. This bears all the hallmarks of that clean, aristocratic style and with its *scherzando* direction, small phrases and energised mood feels akin to a finale.

There are many types of *staccato* and Camidge seems to be asking for a variety here. Looking at bar 6, we see that the first quaver is unmarked, but the second has a *staccato* dot. This is not arbitrary: the first is the end of a phrase, whereas the second is a definite upbeat, synchronised with the bass, to take us to the imperfect cadence. Give more point, more edge to the second – that pinging of a glass, where contact is minimal but lively to make it ring. Although not marked, the *appoggiatura* in bar 18 should be slurred and it would make sense to allow the cadenza to *diminuendo* into the return of the opening material. The *a piacere* crotchets here need shaping;

I find words help to give direction and purpose ('so can you guess what I will play next' for instance). The whole movement needs to be light-hearted, fun. Keep that spirit in the p, contained excitement or anticipation, and imagine extra instruments joining for the louder sections, joyous, cheeky but not forced in tone.

Alwyn   There Sleeps Titania   page 8

'I know a bank where the wild thyme blows' sings Oberon to Puck in *A Midsummer Night's Dream* as he asks him to pour a magic potion on to Titania's eyes. Oxlips, violets, woodbine, eglantine and sweet musk-roses grow in this place, and 'There sleeps Titania sometime of the night / Lull'd in these flowers with dances and delight.' One of the most famous settings of this text is by Alwyn's friend and colleague Benjamin Britten, who famously wrote the role of Oberon for countertenor Alfred Deller. William Alwyn is probably best known now for his film scores, although gradually more of his songs are being programmed. This is a delicate, imaginative and unusual miniature and hopefully may lead us all to explore more of Alwyn's works.

Alwyn has beautifully captured the perfumed dream world of this speech. Time stops as gentle wafts of scent float over Titania's sleep. The potion is dropped, the spell cast in the *molto tranquillo*, then Puck fades away again and we wait for it to work its magic. The phrasing in the LH is a suggestion, an indication that the music should not feel static, but move in breaths within the pedal. As I've mentioned for several other pieces, it is often more difficult to lift the pedal completely for two or three notes, than to continue discreet *legato* pedalling. Ask yourself whether a complete change of colour and texture is really what is wanted in the moments where pedal is not indicated – probably not in bar 6, but maybe in bars 10-14. Your decision, but don't put extra pedal in if you are not confident about not blurring consecutive notes in a lower tessitura. Playing the thirds *legato* is perfectly possible if you employ some sleight of hand and take a few notes in the LH in bars 10, 12 & 25. Find a special sound for the pp in bar 26, perhaps with the help of the *una corda*. You need to cast a spell over your audience when you perform this. Before you begin imagine the scene with Titania asleep amongst the flowers. Listen to the quality of silence, hear those first two bars in your head, then gently, gently begin to play...

Járdányi   Andantino (from *Sonatina no. 2*)   page 10

This is a genial but rather uneventful piece. The writing is detailed and quite transparent, so it will be a matter of careful study of the score, incorporating all marks of dynamic and articulation into a moderately paced performance. Two main themes, one lyrical and one that is more *scherzando*. The first returns in a quasi-development section at bar 33. Both hands cover the same notes an octave apart, but aim to show the different phrasing in each – probably the trickiest moment and it is with relief that the hands begin to synchronise phrasing in bar 39. The *scherzando* theme, first heard from bar 9, is accompanied by a repeated motif. Note the phrasing detail in bar 13 and then in bar 43, as the LH passes the accompaniment to the top part and takes over the main voice. Unusual dynamics here, but clearly intentional. As the hands follow each other down the keyboard in bars 65-68, again show the overlapping phrasing, small stresses on the first notes of each new gesture. And it probably goes without saying that the last note in RH is a low G in the bass!

Pál Járdányi, to give him all his accents, was a Hungarian composer who studied with Kodály and continued that composer's work on collecting folk melodies and using them as the basis for new works. The second theme here definitely sounds as though it were inspired by a folk tune. The whole piece is unfussy and direct; a twentieth century composer wearing the garments of an earlier, more objective, age.

Cornick **Blues for Beth** page 12

Mike Cornick's writing is so imaginative and this Blues is a delight to play – that is, once you have mastered the rhythmic intricacies. Enormous precision is needed here, despite the easy-going swung rhythms, and the instances where he asks pianists to sustain rather than release final notes, as in bar 2, seem almost purposely to be there to confuse! Notice too the difference in articulation between the two hands from bar 9 onwards, with the RH articulating on top of the LH slur, then releasing together. Just to add one more complication, some ends of slurs are accented and some are not. So if you think you are picking the easy jazzy option, think again!

The basic elements of the blues are there, with the flattened thirds and sevenths and the largely I, IV, V harmonies. But the mood is upbeat and positive, with a definite emphasis on fun, on wrong-footing the performer and listener. It will be important to assimilate the rhythmic and articulation details, without extraneous tension. The concentration needed, the sudden stops and starts, can all lead to bad physiological habits, so do keep an eye on this. Working away from the instrument, playing on a table top, or vocalising are good ways of internalising the details before returning to the piano to add in the notes. Those offbeat accents will be helped by small arm thrusts, pushing in and up through a supple wrist, and feel the RH dividing in bar 1, leaning on the fifth finger to sustain the A while the lower fingers are light and active for the triplet. Ultimately this must sound effortless, but of course that takes many hours of effort to achieve.

Pustilnik **Circus Theme** page 15

Fishel Pustilnik has an interesting biography, working mostly in the jazz and popular music fields and composing many educational works using these styles. This *Circus Theme* is based on a stride bass, and the difficulty of the LH makes it appropriate for this level, although in reality there is relatively little substance here in comparison to many of the alternatives.

Learn the chords without the bass notes to begin with. You want to be able to find these easily and it will help if you understand them theoretically as well. Put the bass in and find an easy swing between bass and chord; you should always know where you are moving to before you begin moving, otherwise tension sets in and the sound will become hard. Pedal throughout, generally changing with each minim, sustaining the bass notes, but ensuring that the RH projects well and avoids sounding blurred. Try singing the theme on top when you practise, shaping the bass with the melody. The theme itself is memorable and fun to play. Use some arm to help with the sixths, remember that all quavers are swung, and play both repeats in the exam.

Proksch **And Now Let's Handel** page 16

German composer Michael Proksch has written several volumes of pedagogical music; this comes from *Piano Poetry* and has a rather fun original title of *Jetzt wird geHändelt*. There are a few basic techniques being practised here, primarily the constant quavers, which will be played with the help of some rotary movement, but the extended broken chords in the LH and some varied pedalling are also useful elements to cover.

Firstly, pedalling. There are various possibilities here but what should inform your choices are the range at which the quavers are being played and the direction in bar 26a to only slightly stress the middle voice. The former will mean that you should change the pedal every crotchet when the quavers are in the bass, from bar 9, although you can also play this section without pedal. My instinct would be to stress the middle voice more in the earlier sections, using the pedal to vary the texture. At the opening try pedalling with every minim, or every crotchet, making the sound clearer and more even in the right hand. Then from 25a try changing just once per bar, deliberately making the middle, descending voice more misty, and keeping all else in the background – a dreamy effect which is nothing like Handel, but seems to be what Proksch is requesting here!

The cycle of fifths used here is a useful opportunity for some improvisation. The dynamics are not particularly interesting, but you may like to add a *diminuendo*, or a *crescendo*, at the end.

Balch   A Walk at Strumble Head   page 18

Strumble Head is a rocky headland that forms part of the Pembrokeshire Coast National Park. This evocative piece gives the impression of views over the sea, gulls soaring overhead, gently rippling waves and the odd rougher splash of the tide against the rocks. A sophisticated choice that needs imagination and confident pedalling.

There are various places where you could consider redistributing between the hands. The penultimate bar is a perfect example, allowing more sure control over the *p* dynamic, but the opening whirling of the birds or the wind, and some of the regular, determined dotted crotchet footsteps could also benefit from being shared. This is such a useful skill to develop; we should always do it for musical reasons, but if it aids fluency, evenness, *legato*, as well as making it easier, then why not?

There are a few places that Balch has indicated to be played without pedal. When you start using it again, be sure to depress just after the downbeat to avoid catching the previous notes in the pedal. Similarly be definite about when RH phrases end, so the last F in bar 7 should release before the next pedal, whereas the F in bar 48 sustains for two beats. Bar 40: bring the pedal back once the detached accented Fs have had a chance to be heard as such. A small *crescendo* in bars 27-28 allow the D minor chord to sound enough to fade into the Db major in bar 31 – hear the connection between them. The RH melody often soars, like one's spirits on a good walk, and in other places, bars 22-23, it is busy and precise. Keep an ear on the balance between the hands, the melody needing to project above the accompaniment even in *p*. Unusual and well worth getting to know.

Alexander   All is Calm   page 22

This is both atmospheric and full of a variety of material, with subtle changes in sound world and expressions. Excellent fare to develop sensitive playing, listening and imagination in young pianists, and a piece that will comfortably bear repetition. Even the key is well-chosen, Ab unusual enough to be interesting and useful, and Db of course fitting so well under the fingers for this sort of evocative music.

After paying those compliments to Dennis Alexander I admit I'm not sure how necessary the hand-crossing is in the opening bars. It's a long way up for the LH, destabilising the body, and the RH has plenty of time to get there. Remember when you start that two bars later you need to repeat at a lower dynamic level, so give yourself room for that. Pedalling is meticulously marked – don't miss the *una corda* and *tre corde* that are in very small print – and hopefully pianists will be able to do this quite instinctively by now. Bars 24 & 25 could do with one more change perhaps to clear the consecutive, melodic LH notes, but it is not essential. There is always a danger that pianists rely on the pedal to make the *legato* for them, and this should be guarded against. Practise without pedal to check that the fingers really are linking the notes as much as is possible. The pedal here is creating atmosphere by merging harmonies, blurring the edges, like Da Vinci's *sfumato* technique, but we do still need to balance the layers of texture within that. Keep listening – is that top voice projecting enough through the haze of pedal? Is the accompaniment too prominent? Try also orchestrating the music to imagine the colours you want. There's a magical moment in bar 15, quite celeste-like, that wants clear, precise fingers even in *pp*. We need to hear all six notes one after another in the gently arpeggiated chord at the end and try playing the second chord in the last bar *within* the volume of the first, holding the pedal and slowly pushing that last chord away from you. An evening piece and a perfect one with which to end your practice.

J S Bach	Gavotte en Rondeau (from *Overture in G minor*)	*Schott*

This gavotte is the third movement from a G minor harpsichord suite, BWV 822. It is a sophisticated choice, a good edition presenting you with choices to be made about articulation, dynamics and ornamentation. The main rondo theme returns twice and is basically unaltered, while there are two contrasting sections in Bb major and D minor. Interestingly every 8-bar section follows a similar pattern, with its opening gesture initially leading to an imperfect cadence, then returning, to finish on a perfect cadence. This symmetry is perhaps evidence of its being an early work, but also suits the gavotte, with its minim upbeats and split common time. A tempo of ♩ = c. 60 will keep it moving without haste.

There are many ways of approaching Bach, so my suggestions here are simply one option. Keep the dynamic scheme unfussy. The first interlude in Bb needs a brighter colour and you could imitate the lute stop on one of the repeats of the theme. Baroque players sometimes employ *notes inégales*, an expressive device whereby important notes may be slightly lengthened. On the piano we can achieve the same effect through dynamic and the series of *appoggiaturas* in bars 2-3 would benefit from this, emphasising the dissonance as Bach illegally works his way down the parallel triads! Articulation is possibly where most variety is possible. The first decision will be with or without pedal. If pedal is used, it must be discreet and not blur what are often middle range textures, with much stepwise movement. Consider adding texture and interest by, for instance, detaching the bass crotchets in the first 2 bars, also releasing the thirds with the RH second quaver in bars 2-3. You could also detach the middle voice quavers in bars 10-11, which will differentiate them from the more singing top voice – a similar situation occurs in the D minor section in the LH. A useful trick for the thirds in bar 9 is to angle the hand so that the fourth finger moves *under* finger 3 on the final third, maintaining the *legato*. At this level ornamentation is not essential, but a small cadential trill in the rondo theme, beginning on the upper note, is possible, the three note chords could be gently spread on the beat, and perhaps add an *appoggiatura* at the beginning of bar 28.

Bartók	Romanian Polka	*Universal*

This is the fifth in a group of six *Romanian Folk Dances*, and usually segues straight into the furiously fast finale. This is Bartók's own transcription of original folk melodies, although they are probably more often heard in the version for violin and piano, or for string orchestra. Bartók always included his own metronome marks and timings, but 146 is quite ambitious for this level, and something played with character but nearer 120 would be acceptable.

The pedal markings are also Bartók's own and not so easy to co-ordinate. The main things to notice are the long pedal at the beginning and the lack of pedal in bars 23-24; the first works because of the unchanging LH and the second is necessary for clarity with both hands in a low range. The rest split into two or three alternatives. One is where you change for each crotchet, as in bars 11-12 and 14-15, and the most frequent pedalling groups the $\frac{3}{4}$ bar into 2 + 1, often matching the accents, as in bars 20-21, etc. Employing *legato* pedalling, but with these differentiations will work very well. The markings imply gaps between depression and release of the pedal, but this is not essential here. There is a mixture of $\frac{2}{4}$ and $\frac{3}{4}$, which is not unusual for Bartók. When he transcribed folk material he found it didn't always fit neatly into our neatly classical $\frac{4}{4}$ bar lengths – some 'bars' seemed longer, some shorter. So the way he notated this unevenness was to vary the length of a beat, sometimes filling it with two quavers, sometimes with three. The $\frac{2}{4}$ bars here often come at the end of phrases and seem to work in this way. Don't hang around, but there is no need to hurry through them either; feel the sense of cadence, the extra stress on the *sforzandos*. Two beats, yes, but two longish ones!

The whole thing is based on three-bar phrases, two beginning in D, two on G, then the same again varied, ending on a dominant (that then resolves at the beginning of no. 6). It is quite rough and raucous, spirited and vigorous. The *acciaccaturas* will need to be tightly crushed and the balance carefully controlled so that the top part always projects. Remember that as a performer it is your job to make us excited, but not necessarily be excited yourself. You need a cool head to perform this – stay in control, hold the tempo and play $\boldsymbol{f}$ not $\boldsymbol{ff}$.

Benda	Sonatine in F major	*Schott*

This is standard fare for young pianists, practising all the elements of an early classical style. Neat fingerwork in broken chords and scales played with rhythmic poise and buoyancy will go a long way to making this a success. Benda has made a few suggestions about articulation, but leaves other aspects of interpretation to the performer. This style is also concerned with restraint and a tempo of ♩ = 108 allows precision without hurry. No repeats for the exam.

The opening bars return a few times, sometimes an octave higher, so an opportunity for some dynamic contrast perhaps, but always with a sense of bar 1 moving towards bar 2, which then relaxes into the cadence – show this through sound rather than pulse. The bass should play bar 2 non-*legato*. Bars 5-6 are written to be played between the hands, but feel free to experiment with just using RH, with the sense of the bar making a *diminuendo* from the bass note. This continual moulding of the dynamic level keeps the music alive and in the classical style is largely governed by the harmony. Benda has neatly turned the end of the first section into the first bar of the second. Here too consider separating the bass broken chord quavers, making a small *crescendo* into the crotchets and the next RH gesture. I suggest playing the *acciaccaturas* as semiquavers on the beat, observing the slurs. In bar 28 there is a link into a brief minor moment, which you can highlight through sound. Apart from these two bars. the movement is bright and sunny, so just a small *rit.* to end with grace. No masterpiece, but fresh, affable and rather cleansing to play.

Diabelli	Moderato cantabile (from *Sonatina in F major*)	*Alfred*

Alas poor Diabelli. Beethoven knew him well and his name will forever be linked in pianists' minds with the story behind Beethoven's *Diabelli Variations*. Diabelli had sent 50 composers a waltz he'd written, hoping that each would contribute a variation he could then publish. Beethoven was initially very disparaging about the waltz and refused to join the enterprise, but finally wrote 33 variations, which formed one of his great masterpieces for the piano. I suspect that this sonatina was written as teaching material and it takes a step further towards the romantic period than the previous sonatine by Benda. More expressive, with more variety of characterisation, but still needing an understanding of the classical style and its pianistic requirements. A crotchet pulse of 112 works well.

The opening seven bars form the first subject material, to be played *cantabile*, the arm helping to add depth to the sound, probably with pedal, and with a careful balance between melody and accompaniment. By bar 8 we are in the dominant and the mood changes to something more playful and cheeky. I suggest detaching the LH quavers here, until the slur in bar 11, and finding a crisper, lighter sound quality. The development also plays with this contrast, beginning lyrically, with more minor inflected *appoggiaturas*, before a *crescendo* leads to a ***ff*** climax (a classical ***ff*** only please), a dash up the keyboard and halting return to the opening music. Notice the dynamic change here (although strangely Diabelli adjusts the RH dynamic but not the LH's) and in bar 35 I would play *legato* for the bass last four quavers as in bar 11. Keep the energy and tempo for the final chords so that the tension falls into the pause on the rest at the end.

Fonteyn   Pop Looks Bach   *Boosey*

Apparently Sam Fonteyn told his son that if he'd known this piece was to become so famous, he'd have called it something else. But most of us will recognise it as the theme to *Ski Sunday*, albeit orchestrated for TV. Fonteyn was a prolific composer for the Boosey & Hawkes Music Library, and various TV shows chose his music for their theme tunes. *Please Sir!* was one of his, as was the theme for Barbara Woodhouse's dog training programmes. He may get more street cred from those of a younger vintage if we also mention his *Galloping Gertie* has featured in *SpongeBob SquarePants*...

Musically this is straightforward, demanding a high level of energy to be maintained throughout. Listening to the orchestrated version will give you ideas about colour, and remember to hold something in reserve for the *crescendo* and ***ff*** at the very end. It may also encourage you to play it a little faster than marked. Around 88 is suitable, but making sure the quavers are well in control and do not hurry. Technically these continual quavers in the RH will need careful practice, with the aim not just of learning the notes, but of playing them with firm fingers but a supple wrist. Use arm weight to help you play the chords, but once the quavers begin you can use some rotary motion, keeping the fingers active, unencumbered by pressure from the arm. It also helps to give the bass attention, shaping those slurred phrases, articulating the upbeat to bar 11, and generally allowing it to take the musical lead.

The character changes in bar 27, with the whole orchestra playing chords together, followed by a solo instrument being given a new theme. The warm sound of a saxophone? a brighter, edgier trumpet? Use your imagination to find a different tone colour here. No former experience in skiing required, but a considerable pianistic challenge.

Kabalevsky   Cavalryman (no. 20 from *Thirty Children's Pieces*, op. 27)   *Boosey*

Please don't be put off by the key signature of Bb minor or the instruction to play it *Allegro molto* (around ♩ = 108 will do); this is a splendid, dramatic gallop cross the steppes that should fire the imagination of many pianists. Kabalevsky's children's pieces are a treasure trove for teachers and students alike.

Much detail to be noted and incorporated into a performance. Work on the primary triads in Bb minor and V⁷ – I in F major. One unusual chord in the penultimate bar (I would play the Fb in the LH, leaving RH with a chord of Gb) and you're set to go. Notice that the chords themselves are *f* only for the introductory bars each time they occur, but then fade into the background over the melody. The *p* is missing in the recapitulation, but you'll probably want to do the same in bars 46 & 56. Great to have a melody in the bass, and such a strong one too, putting the LH through its paces. Listen for a tight dotted rhythm, making sure you use strong fingers in those places to be in control. The semiquaver needs substance; these are fighting men, so it may be temporally short, but should not sound light. The motif always leads into the second bar, the *tenuto* and the chord of IV, so begin in a way that makes that possible, ie without a bump on the first Bb in bar 3. Show the difference between the accented, longer quavers in bar 8 and the identical notes played with a feisty *staccato* in the following bar.

Of course, these are Cossacks, so there is melancholy here too, and this comes in the middle section. Lean on the *tenutos* in bars 21-23; no longer the fierce f of the opening, but something more weighty, more deeply sorrowful in the colour. The hands change roles, with the arm helping the top line to sing richly while lower fingers remain light and nimble for the accompanying chords. Some rearranging will make bar 38 easier, taking the middle voice F into the LH (you can do this for a few bars if you wish). Throughout the piece you have these offbeat chords. They depict the idea of being on horseback, that bounce while you are on the horse, and they also signify the relentlessness of the gallop. Keep this one moving right up to the final explosive chord.

Norton   Kettle Rag   *Trinity*

Ragtime piano originated in America around the turn of the twentieth century, and was made famous by Scott Joplin. Christopher Norton's bright and breezy *Kettle Rag* features LH chords on the weak second beat of the bar, the blue note (the major and minor third of the key in alternation, such as the B and Bb in bars 1-2, the E and Eb in bar 17, etc) and a syncopated feeling throughout. The piece may be played at a tempo of ♩ = c. 132 (rather than ♩ = 150).

Play the LH very rhythmically, the *staccato* crotchets dry and punchy. In the RH, carefully observe all *staccato* notes, and shorten the second note in the slurred pairs. Exaggerate all the accents, especially those that come on weak beats.

Petot   The Newtonville Bounce   *Kjos*

Bounce music originally hails from New Orleans and is energetic and related to hip hop. Ross Petot is an American pianist and composer specialising in jazz and ragtime. He teaches in Newton, Massachusetts, hence the title. The tempo is brisk (♩ = 152) but the mood, with its swung quavers and offbeat stresses, is relatively relaxed and easy-going, evoking memories of the 1920s and the flapper generation.

Watch out for the reversion to Bb in LH bar 12 & 33 (cautionary accidentals have not been used). Many of the chords here are unusual, so do spend time getting to know them, finding a comfortable position for the hand, moving into the keyboard rather than twisting for black notes, and deciding on the physical action that will give you a weighted *staccato*. The slurs in bars 3-4 and 27-29 are not really possible, but you can link one or two notes. Notice the LH *legato* from 28-29, which can be done.

The rest is self-explanatory. Enjoy the moments when the bass plays something other than the offbeat chords, and you will probably want to vary tone colour a little during the piece. Lightweight, nonchalant, and very enjoyable.

Shostakovich   Gavotte   *Boosey*

Famously, there are few photographs of Shostakovich that show him smiling, yet there are many works, such as this Gavotte, that contain much wit and humour. These *Dolls' Dances* were originally movements from his *Ballet Suites* for orchestra, but are beautifully arranged for young pianists, all extraneous notes expunged, so that a clean, pseudo-classical texture is all that remains. This idea of mechanical dolls dancing makes the offbeat accents and sudden sleight of hand move into Db all the more amusing.

Slurs are carefully marked and classically imply both an emphasis of the first note in the slur and a lifting of the last. Experiment with articulation elsewhere, perhaps finding a warmer, less clipped *detaché* (walking *en pointe* perhaps) for the opening crotchets and something altogether more crisp (a *battement*?) when marked *staccato* as in bars 17 & 18. There are one or two moments that would benefit from the sustaining pedal: the fourth beat accents in bars 36, 40, etc to give added sonority and incongruity, and to help with the *legato* in bars 35 & 36. Once set, the tempo should be more or less constant, but unhurried, poised, hearing space around the upbeats to new sections to allow the dancers to breathe and re-group (for instance in bars 8 & 16). Find a new colour for the A minor section, more muted shades and a heavier texture with the sustained drone-like basses. Only a slight slowing up at the end – this is no deflating Olympia, but a long-life battery operated prim ballerina, ending with a final pirouette. Around ♩ = 138.

Vine   Semplice (from *Red Blues*)   *Faber*

Carl Vine is both a celebrated and prolific Australian composer. He has written many larger scale orchestral works, but his *Five Bagatelles* and *Piano Sonata* are firm favourites amongst pianists. This rather touching Semplice comes from a collection of four pieces, *Red Blues*. It needs confident pedalling and sensitive musicianship. Yes, the changing bar lengths are a little disconcerting at first but the shape of the phrases fits them very naturally.

Although pedalling is essential, do practise without to feel the *legato*, the shapes, under your fingers. *Legato* on the piano is of course a problematic concept, with a strong argument to be made that it is the balancing of sound rather than the linking of fingers (within pedal) that is more important. However, the writing here is linear and melodic – the bass too has melodic elements, resolving dissonances, within its arpeggiations – so developing the technique of walking from one note to the other, transferring weight and shaping the line en route is important. Interestingly Vine has given us *mp* at the beginning and nothing else until the last line. He is suggesting that the mood is intimate, coaxing, almost hesitant with the many rests, but while keeping within that frame, there will inevitably be a variety of tone colours and a gentle dynamic following of the shape of the lines. So the plethora of sharps from bar 9 will bring a new energy; the return at bar 17 – should this be less or more than the opening? Bar 3 seems to reach further than bar 1...it is good to see that composers trust performers to make their own decisions.

Once the *legato* is fully ingrained, add the pedal, noticing where both hands have a rest and there should be a break in the sound, and where the LH only lifts. I find following the pedalling exactly as marked more difficult than to use it throughout. Either option is fine as long as the result observes both the rests and the long marked pedals, but if you do depress at the beginning of bars (rather than change, which is lift then depress), take care not to catch the last note of the previous bar in the pedal. Bar 25: the B should sound alone before the long pedal through the following bar.

Grades 6-8

At Grades 6-8, candidates will typically be able consciously to integrate their skills, knowledge and understanding in a secure and sustained performance which demonstrates mature grasp of the material. Along with confidence, a sense of ownership and self-awareness, this will result in a discriminating and sensitive personal interpretation that conveys complexity and control of shape (eg throughout a sonata movement), and awareness of stylistic interpretation. The performance will be grounded in thorough and relevant preparation, and will demonstrate authority and control. Candidates will combine skilful and appropriate command with imaginative response and flair to engage the audience wholeheartedly.

These features will be demonstrated through material largely drawn from the standard repertoire for the instrument. Overall length will be sufficient to enable variety and range of presentation to be demonstrated and sustained. Content will be substantial, with some depth and sophistication, enabling the candidate to engage with complex emotions and abstract musical thought. It will be such as to require analysis and reflection in the preparation, and present challenging physical requirements in one or more technical aspects. The musical language may demand considerable inferential understanding and thoughtful interpretation to reflect subtlety of meaning (eg contrapuntal texture, musical irony or humour).

Grade 6

Group A

| Byrd | Coranto (no. 218 from *Fitzwilliam Virginal Book*) | page 2 |

William Byrd was an English composer of the Renaissance period, remembered for his church music, choral works, consort music and pieces for keyboard. This *Coranto* is among his many contributions to an important collection of keyboard music from the late Elizabethan and early Jacobean periods, known as *The Fitzwilliam Virginal Book*. A virginal (or virginals) is a rectangular type of harpsichord, smaller and simpler in construction. The sound is produced by quills that pluck the strings, creating a crisp and incisive tone quality.

A *Coranto* is a type of triple-metre dance common in instrumental music from the period (the title literally means 'running'). This example is lively in spirit, and needs to be articulated cleanly, especially with regard to the ornaments (indicated here with diagonal slashes through the note stems). It is advisable to practise the piece without the ornaments at first, adding them in very lightly only when you have developed some fluency. Ornaments are played on the beat. A non-*legato* touch is best suited to this piece, with clear punctuation at the end of each phrase. Gently separate the longer notes and play the running quaver passages cleanly, using a touch that is well articulated from the fingers. Chords may be arpeggiated quickly, holding on to each note by hand for the full duration. Composers in Byrd's day did not use phrase marks to show where the breathing places fell – see if you can find where each phrase ends and the next one begins. The dynamic markings are editorial suggestions appropriate to the style when played on the piano. No pedal is necessary.

J S Bach   Prelude in D minor, BWV 635   page 4

Bach wrote a number of pieces for his own teaching purposes. The *Prelude in D minor* comes from a set of six familiarly known as the 'Little Preludes'. It is in the style of a two-part invention, a duet between the two hands in which both hands are of equal importance.

The main subject (bar 1, etc) consists of three notes that move by step followed by three notes that move by skip. It is effective to play the steps more *legato* and the skips more detached. Experiment with mixing up *legato* and non-*legato* touches, allowing the line to breathe at phrase ends. You will want to add subtle *crescendo-diminuendo* hairpins to shape the semiquaver lines; quavers sound best when played with a bouncy *staccato* to bring out the dance quality of the piece. Fit the right-hand ornaments (bars 4 and 23 together with the LH precisely (ornaments come on the beat); isolate these two bars regularly in your practice and work on them patiently. Begin your work at a slow tempo with each hand separately before you put the hands together. Practise in very small sections of one bar, stopping on the first note of the next bar. Repeat two or three times in a row with full concentration so you form good habits and avoid errors. It is most important for eventual security in performance that you organise a good fingering that suits your hand, and stick to it each and every time you practise (the fingering given here is a guide only). Thereafter you can work in two- and then four-bar units, progressing to larger sections. Even after you can play the piece fluently with both hands it is advisable to play each hand separately on occasion, listening for evenness in the semiquaver patterns as you shape and articulate the lines.

Benda   Sonatina in E flat   page 6

Georg Benda was a prolific composer of the early Classical period, a Czech émigré who lived and worked in Germany. He wrote religious works and melodramas in addition to much instrumental music, including 34 sonatinas for piano or harpsichord. The *Sonatina in E flat* is a concise model of sonata form in miniature, an ideal preparation for the sonatas of the Classical masters. The first subject is smoothly flowing and gently expressive; the second subject (from bar 17) starts with an energetic, angular dotted theme that soon gives way to a drooping phrase and a mood of pathos at the interrupted cadence in bar 24. Notice how Benda writes a varied repeat of the second theme, this time resolving into the dominant key in bar 31. The development section (after the double bar) combines features of both first and second themes, touching on the minor keys of F and G. The recapitulation (bar 63) obeys the rules of sonata form by presenting the second subject material (from bar 79) in the home key.

The *Allegretto* marking tells us to move forwards while allowing time for the expressive moments. Taper off phrase endings, short slurs and *appoggiaturas* beautifully, and take time over *fermatas* and other special moments of repose (bars 24, 82). In keeping with the style of the period sharp dotted rhythms can be broken, the dot becoming a rest. This will certainly help with the shifts in position in bars 17 and 18, etc. Make the most of all the contrasts in dynamics and texture, and feel the many changes in mood in character.

Jones   Giga in A minor   page 10

Not much is known about the life of English baroque composer, Richard Jones. Like many of his contemporaries, he was overshadowed by the popularity of Handel whose music was all the rage in England at the time. In 1732 Jones produced six sets of *Lessons for the Harpsichord or Spinet*, which are charming suites of dance movements composed for instructional purposes. The *Giga* (*Jig*) is the final movement of the *Fourth Lesson*, featuring pieces in the key of A minor.

A jig is a lively dance in compound meter, and in this example in $^{12}_{8}$ we need to feel the four main dotted crotchet beats in each bar. The suggested articulations for the quaver groups really help the music to dance; make a small separation between the note at the end of the slur and the note that follows. Notes without any articulation markings may be played *legato* or detached (slightly shorter than the written value), or a mixture of the two at the performer's choice. For example, you might prefer to join the dotted crotchets in the LH (bars 3, 5, etc) and detach the skipping crotchet-quaver patterns (RH bar 1; LH bar 2, etc) for contrast and rhythmic variety. There is no one right way to do this; experiment with touch and articulation until you find the way that suits you. Like the majority of dance movements from suites of this period, the *Giga* is in binary form. The music modulates to the dominant minor key at the end of the first half, and returns to the home key via the relative major (notice the cadence in C major in bar 15). All ornaments are to be played on the beat.

C P E Bach   Solo per il Cembalo (Allegro), BWV Anh 129   *Bärenreiter*

C P E Bach was the second son of J S Bach, and an important composer, theorist and keyboard player. This energetic piece in the *galant* style is in binary form, the first half taking the music from the tonic key (Eb) to the dominant key (Bb) and the second half back to the tonic. If the first half proceeds directly to its destination, the music takes an indirect and altogether more scenic route home.

It is a musicianly quality to know what key we are playing in at any given moment, and therefore worth the effort to identify the main key areas the music visits from bar 21. Originally written for the harpsichord or clavichord, when playing this piece on the piano we need to remember to add dynamics and articulation so that the music can come to life. We decide on the dynamics based on the character of the music as we feel it, the patterns and shapes we discover and the direction of the harmony informing our choices (an echo effect in bar 52 is there for the taking). Just as there is no such thing as the one correct tempo, there is also some leeway in matters of articulation. In an *allegro* movement such as this it is appropriate to detach the quavers lightly, except in the falling ornamented pairs in the right hand (bar 6, etc); the *appoggiatura* and its resolution are played joined by a slur. Semiquaver patterns are melodic and will respond to a well-shaped and contoured *legato* touch; play the triplet semiquavers somewhat lighter. Ornaments begin on the beat; the short trills consist of four notes and start on the upper note (even if this means repeating the note just before the ornament). To preserve clarity of line and texture, no pedal is necessary.

Dušek   Allegro (from *Sonata no. 3 in B flat major*)   *Bärenreiter*

František Xaver Dušek (1731–1799) was a Czech composer, harpsichordist and pianist. *Sonata no. 3* is an excellent example of a Classical style sonata form movement; a successful performance relies on an understanding of stylistic practices, especially with regard to dynamics, articulation and ornamentation. In this period ornaments come on the beat, trills starting from the upper note; the short trills (indicated by the wavy line without the vertical stroke) ideally comprise four notes (upper-main-upper-main) but due to the fast tempo (*allegro* with an *alla breve* time signature) a three-note ornament (main-upper-main) or even an *acciaccatura* may be more realistic alternatives, depending on the technical ability of the player. The ornament in bar 25 (etc) indicates a trill with a termination; the trill in bar 10, for example, needs no termination. Dušek has left the choice of dynamics and articulation up to the performer. A suggested plan is to begin brightly, *mf* with crotchets lightly detached; from bar 6 the mood is more expressive, calling for a *legato* touch and a drop in the dynamic level. Make a *crescendo* from bar 10 to 13, then suddenly softer, accenting the first of each left-hand triplet group to point the bass line. The second subject (from bar 18) might be played strongly with an extravert character or softer and more delicately, using a *leggiero* touch for the semiquavers. Experiment and find out which way works better for you, remembering that there is no such thing as the one correct solution.

Schubert   Scherzo in B flat major, D 593 no.1   *Henle*

Schubert wrote this *Scherzo* in 1817. The shape of the piece is ternary form (ABA), each section itself in two halves. A successful performance requires responsiveness to harmonic colour (there are some surprising twists), rhythmic poise and control of sound and texture.

The title literally means 'joke' but the *allegretto* indication warns us not to take too fast a tempo. The Viennese rhythmic character requires stylish handling of the metre. While the ability to maintain a steady pulse is an essential skill for any musician, a foursquare performance of this piece would be extremely dull, and for this reason overuse of the metronome is not recommended. In the opening phrases the first beats of each bar are much stronger than the second beats, but the high points of the phrases are the accented slurs, which must receive the biggest stresses (bars 4, 8, 12, etc). Take a moment to linger on these notes, enjoying the dissonance before resolving very lightly on the quavers that follow. Schubert's *fortissimos* tend not to be as heavy or dramatic as Beethoven's; keep the sound round in bars 13-14, adding touches of pedal for resonance. There is a very beautiful muting of the colour scheme from bar 20, the modulation to the remote key of Db calling for a sudden drop to *pp*. The trio is in the subdominant key (Eb), darker and more relaxed in character with a contrast in texture. The left-hand accents on the (otherwise weak) second beats add rhythmical interest but should not obscure the melodic line. The meandering quaver line in the left hand (from bar 67) is the darkest point in the work, requiring melodic shaping and, because of the low register, clarity of articulation and minimal pedal.

Telemann   Allegro (from *Fantasia no. 1 in D major*)   *Schott*

Telemann was a contemporary of Bach, Handel and Scarlatti, and an extremely prolific composer. This *Fantasia* in ternary form, in which both hands play an equal role, requires control of finger work at a fast tempo while maintaining a rock-steady pulse. You may desire a slight broadening of the tempo in the closing two bars; elsewhere, keep strictly in time. The *Fantasia* is an excellent piece for reinforcing the teaching of key relationships, since the main key areas associated with D major are very clearly presented; the dominant (bar 22), the subdominant (bar 23), and the relative minor (bar 34).

Telemann left no dynamic instructions but of course we need to supply our own in performance. D major is a bright key, but the $\frac{3}{8}$ time signature suggests a certain lightness. A dynamic level of *mf* works well for the outer sections; the B section may be played more softly to create light and shade. Rising sequences suggest a *crescendo* (bars 9-12; 43-46); echo effects (bars 7-8, etc) may be played as softly as possible as long as the tempo and clarity of execution are sustained.

Semiquavers are best played with clearly articulated finger work, somewhere between *legato* and *staccato*; quavers may be lightly detached or joined, the choice is up to the individual performer. If you settle on a more *legato* approach, you might still prefer to detach the left-hand quavers at the end of the phrases (bar 4, etc). Make sure the triplet semiquavers do not slow you down; a lighter touch is suitable here (bars 19-20, etc). Punctuate the different sections by inserting a small articulation (before bars 23 and 40), as well as before the echo effects (bars 29 and 59).

Group B

Karganov   Arabesque page 12

Genary Karganov was a Russian composer known for his instructional piano compositions. This delightful late Romantic *Arabesque* is full of tender expression, demanding sensitivity of touch, timing, and pedalling as well as control of texture and balance between the hands.

Observe the rests in the right hand in bars 2 and 3, to keep the next harmony clean and the composer's breaks in the melodic line clear. The minim note heads on the first beats in the left hand tell us to add a little more weight to the bass notes, playing the harmony notes lighter and phrasing off at the end of the slur. Apart from bars 27 and 28 (where different pedalling is indicated) we hold the pedal for a whole bar, changing on the first note of the next bar (*legato* pedalling). Don't be confused by the *staccato* dots underneath the slurs (bars 6, 10, etc), these markings tell us to play *staccato* in the hand but to keep the pedal down. Many composers in the Romantic period use this type of notation for *rubato* effects and we may take our time over them. The same principle applies to the short right-hand rests (bar 19, etc); make the rest with your hand but continue to hold the pedal down. The dynamic contrasts are very important for expression. The *ppp* from bar 21 requires a very special colour and a dreamy effect; use the left pedal (*una corda*) for this, and take your time. Push forwards at the *f* in bar 25, and take a lot of time at the *ritenuto* in bar 27. *Ritenuto* tells us to slow down with immediate effect; the *rallentando* in the final bar tells us to slow gradually.

Schmitz   Progression I page 14

Manfred Schmitz was a German composer, pianist and teacher who wrote jazz-inspired music for young pianists. *Progression I* comes from his series, *Mini Rock*.

The piece is full of interesting rhythmic effects, requiring considerable independence between the hands in syncopated patterns and the ability to feel metrical shifts against a steady pulse. The time signature is ¢ (*alla breve*), meaning there are two beats in a bar and not four. It might be helpful to get a preliminary sense of how the hands fit together by tapping the rhythmic patterns on your knee or the closed lid of the piano while counting the two beats of the bar out aloud. Notice there are three different note lengths in the right-hand chords in bar 1, etc, a *staccato* crotchet on the first beat followed by a *staccato* quaver (lighter) and then a crotchet tied over the bar line to a semibreve. Accent the syncopation at the end of the bar as marked, keeping your left hand very steady. Articulate the quaver patterns clearly making sure they are even and controlled (the left-hand quavers in bar 2, etc require careful control of the weaker 4th and 5th fingers). There is a neat rhythmical effect in bars 6-8 and 14-16; three quaver groups crossing the regular pulse. Enjoy this as you play! All accents can be exaggerated for rhythmical effect. To preserve the crispness of the *staccatos* and clarity in the articulations at the end of the short phrases, pedal only where indicated.

Ramskill   Weaving a Spell page 17

Robert Ramskill was born in 1950. His compositional style combines jazz influences with classical forms giving his music popular appeal. This charming waltz-like piece begins with a short introduction featuring major seconds on white keys.

The left hand from bar 9 is in two-bar phrases; the pattern of rising and falling fifths evoking a gently lilting or swinging mood on top of which the right hand sings and dances. Gently release the second note of the two-note slurs in the melody line, and pay attention to all marks of articulation.

In the passage from bar 31 pass the line back and forth between the hands seamlessly with no lumps or bumps. The first section (to bar 37) is in the Mixolydian mode (like a major scale but with a flattened seventh; in this case A major with a G♮).

At the start of the second section (from bar 38) the left hand has the melody line; can you identify the chords in the right hand? They are mostly major or minor, but we find a major seventh chord in bar 50 and a chord with a suspension in bar 53. Notice the change of texture at bar 54; the melody returns to the right hand, the left features a line in the outer fingers and a chord on the offbeat. Play the dotted minims more fully (connecting the notes as indicated by the phrase marks), touching in the chord lightly. Enjoy the cross rhythms the slurred quaver groups bring to the coda (the right hand feels like it is playing two dotted crotchet beats in the bar against the three beats in the left hand).

Béra-Tagrine   Mazurka   page 20

Nathalie Béra-Tagrine is a French pianist and composer of educational piano music. A mazurka is a lively folk dance in triple time that originated in Poland, with strong accents on the second or third beats of the bar. Chopin and Szymanowski wrote many; listening to a few examples would make excellent background research for the study of this piece.

There are four eight-bar phrases, the first and third of which are identical in notes and rhythm (the overall shape is ABAC). Articulate all short slurs and longer phrase marks clearly; connect the notes under the slur and ensure a sharp release on the last note. The pedalling in this piece needs careful attention. There are two different types of pedalling marked by the composer, *legato* and direct. In the direct pedals in the opening (bars 1–8, etc), put the pedal down together with the hands, releasing sharply on the third beat. This separates the last beat in the left hand from the first beat in the next bar, but does not always affect the *legato* connection in the right hand (for example, make a *legato* connection in the right hand between bars 2 and 3, and bars 4 and 5, etc). Play those notes marked with *staccato* dots short even when the pedal is down; we hear articulation through the pedal and the *staccato* releases help us play rhythmically. We make a change to *legato* pedalling from bar 9, meaning the foot comes up as the hands go down on the first beat of bar 10, etc. The lower stave from bar 9 needs careful practice with the left hand alone. Notice the descending line in dotted minims; the long notes should be played *legato* and the crotchet chords *staccato*.

In Dreams
Walsh/Shore (from *The Lord of the Rings: The Fellowship of the Ring*) page 22

In Dreams is a song by Howard Shore originally written for the film *The Lord of the Rings: The Fellowship of the Ring*. This is an arrangement for piano by Nicolai Podgornov from his *Romantic Piano Album*. A successful performance calls for the ability to shape and project a melodic line in the top of the right hand while playing chords underneath more softly; a feeling for harmonic colour and control of pedal are also important requirements.

The melody line is always on the top; for clarity and projection voice the right-hand chords to the top note (stems up), playing the underneath notes (stems down) softer. Play changes of harmony softly when they occur underneath a sustained melody note (bars 7, 12, etc), making sure to hold on to the melody note so it is held in the new pedal. It is good practice to play the melody line while shadowing all the notes underneath (touching the keys but aiming not to sound the notes); this is challenging at first but if you persist you will develop your chord voicing technique (a skill transferable to many other pieces). Enjoy the lovely change in colour when a long melody note is harmonised firstly with one chord and then another; the E in bar 13, for example, is at first the fifth degree of the A major chord, then becoming the third degree of the C major chord. The pedalling plan is to make *legato* changes with each new harmony. Observe the longer pedals in bars 2, 4-5, 23 and 36.

Granados Vals Sentimental *Boileau*

Granados was a Spanish pianist and composer who wrote in a uniquely Spanish style. This sentimental waltz is from a set of waltzes entitled *Valses poéticos*, written in 1899. The direction *quasi ad libitum* invites the player to approach the music with a sense of freedom; a generous way with *rubato* and personal feeling are absolutely appropriate. Tone colour, mood and atmosphere are all-important in this piece; take plenty of time to linger over special moments (there are plenty of them throughout). The key of F♯ minor is associated with passion and gloominess; the modulation into the relative major (A, in bar 15) brings a very brief moment of sunshine. We find colour not only in the harmonies but also in the register changes; when the opening theme returns in bar 17 it is more translucent. If you notice this and can savour it, it will communicate to your listeners!

Linger over the grace notes and make them expressive, as you would if you sang them. They come before the beat, except for bar 31 when they are played on the beat together with the left-hand chord (the pedal going down only after the A♯). The top right-hand melody line needs to be beautifully shaped and projected; the left hand requires especial delicacy in the closing section, from bar 33. In general, use pedal generously; a slight mistiness is not only permissible but actually desirable. Bar 2, etc, works well in one pedal because it is one harmony; bar 4 needs three changes. Hold the pedal for two bars in bars 7-8, 23-24, etc. Change with each crotchet beat in bars 11 and 12. The G♯-C♯ (treble stave bars 7-8, etc) may be taken with the left hand crossing over the right.

Kallmeyer Nemi Lounge *DVfM*

Nemi Lounge is from Ulrich Kallmeyer's *Cool Cat Piano Goodies*, a collection of intermediate pieces exploring various pop idioms. The piece is in ternary form (ABA); the *da capo al fine* direction is not optional and must be observed in all performances. Omit the A♭ and B♭ crotchets at the end of bar 11 for the final bar. Don't be intimidated by a key signature of six flats; it is extremely important for the developing pianist to become familiar with all the keys, and this piece offers an excellent opportunity to improve accuracy in reading, especially with the numerous accidentals to watch out for. The home key is Gb major, the middle section ('Enter Caligula') in the dominant key (Db). Because of the extreme chromaticism it is important to learn the notes extremely slowly to make sure you get them right from the outset; errors in notes and rhythm are easily ingrained and extremely difficult to correct afterwards.

The mood is gently lyrical, soft and level throughout the A section; in the B section the right hand needs to sing out above the left hand. Notice that the loudest dynamic marking is only *mf* (bars 18 and 20). A syncopation is where a weak beat or part of a beat is stressed instead of a strong beat (creating rhythmical interest and variety), and this piece is full of them (the first appears in the top line of bar 2). Feeling a pulse of two dotted minim beats per bar rather than six crotchets ($\frac{6}{4}$ is a compound time signature) will help you feel the syncopations as they cross the beats. It is a good idea to practise without pedal at first, aiming to make *legato* connections in the hand wherever possible before adding pedal in later. It is also well worth organising a fingering that enables these connections, and writing it in your score.

Prokofiev Cortège de sauterelles (March of the Grasshoppers) *Boosey*

March of the Grasshoppers is the seventh pieces from Prokofiev's popular set of pieces for children, *Musiques d'enfants*, opus 65, composed in 1935. It is a jaunty march featuring dotted rhythms, unison passages, and left hand jumps; it uses an extensive range of the keyboard, and there are a variety of dynamic levels.

The dotted rhythms that contain semiquaver rests (bar 1, etc) need to be played precisely, the rest clearly audible. Play the dotted rhythms under phrase marks *legato* with a fingering that makes this possible (it is always advisable to write some fingering in the score). While we will want to use touches of pedal for colour and accent throughout the piece, we should not rely on the pedal to make connections. The unison passages in the B section (*poco meno mosso*) pose particular pianistic challenges, namely precision in attack and release and tonal balance between the hands. Play the left hand very slightly softer than the right, listening very carefully that the hands sound absolutely together. Observe the phrasing and articulation marks carefully; crotchets that are not under a phrase mark should be slightly detached (bar 23). The left-hand jumps in the B major section (from bar 33) are also played detached (the *legato* phrase mark applies to the right hand). For security with the jumps, regular practice with the left hand alone is essential (you might even memorise this section and practise with your eyes closed). Punctuate between phrases with a small articulation (bars 8 and 9, for example). Prokofiev has given us the opportunity to paint a comical picture in sound; a convincing performance relies on the ability to build up a vivid picture in the imagination throughout the learning process.

Pütz Raining Cats and Dogs *Schott*

Eduard Pütz was a German composer and music educator. *Raining Cats and Dogs* is from his collection of jazzy pieces, *I'm sorry, Mr. Czerny*. This pieces serves as a study in developing the weaker fingers in the right hand, evenness in passagework, passing a line smoothly from one hand to the other and in maintaining a regular pulse while playing notes and chords off the beat.

Apart from the *poco rit.* in bar 20, a stable pulse is needed throughout. The RH syncopation in bar 2 (etc) followed by the offbeat chord in the left poses a rhythmic challenge that could be helped by the metronome; an alternative is to count aloud while you play until the hands fit together perfectly with (or against) the beat. Make sure the triplets are even and melodically shaped; when they are passed back and forth between the hands (bars 13, 17-18) the transfer needs to feel as smooth and seamless as two runners passing a baton in a relay race. A carefully organised fingering will greatly assist with phrasing and control in general. Enjoy the syncopation produced by the three accented left-hand Cs (bars 17 and 18), grading them carefully within the *diminuendo*. The left-hand tenths (bars 5 and 25) may be broken. Notice the false relation between the hands in bars 11 and 12; the left hand plays A♮ against the right hand's A♭ in the F♯⁹ chords. For clarity of phrasing and articulation, practise with no pedal; in performance, use only very light pedalling.

Reger   Versöhnung (Reconciliation) (from *Aus der Jugendzeit*)   *Trinity*

Allow your imagination to come up with a storyline for what is going on in this delightful late Romantic piece, as though it were the background music to a scene in a film. Feel it as you play. The character asks someone to be their friend again – pleading, commiserating and even dancing to win back their affection.

We need an appropriate sense of *rubato* to bring the necessary rhythmic flexibility to the phrasing. If you sing the melody line, you will soon discover where the breathing places are. Voice the RH to the top in order to project the melody line with a deep, warm *legato*, listening that the lower RH and LH notes do not cover your sound. In bar 4, play the alto part more lightly than the top; in bar 7, the top G♯ needs more depth of tone than the quavers underneath. Attend carefully to the long notes and tied notes in the lower parts, making sure you sustain them for their full length to give harmonic richness. Use pedal with each new change of harmony to add resonance and to help with the joins. The change of mood in the second section (from bar 11) calls for a new tempo as well as a new colour – brighter and a little quicker. Phrase the two-note slurs in the RH energetically over the bouncy LH *staccatos*, feeling how the music now dances. Enjoy the contrast between the solemn character in bars 28-29 and the playful, teasing one in the two bars that follow.

Satie   Gymnopédie no. 3   *Henle*

Erik Satie published the three *Gymnopédies* in 1888; the title refers to an ancient Greek dance rite. Despite its apparent simplicity, *Gymnopédie no. 3* requires control and refinement of tone in soft dynamic levels, projection and shaping of a melodic line over an agile left hand, *legato* pedalling and responsiveness to mood and colour. The tempo is slow, and the atmosphere serious, mournful and hypnotic. There are just two dynamic markings, $\boldsymbol{p}$ and $\boldsymbol{pp}$.

It may be helpful to think in terms of two different tonal levels between the hands – a fuller singing tone for the right hand's luminous singing line (listen carefully for tonal shading in the hairpin *crescendos* and *diminuendos*) and a softer, more transparent sound for the left hand. Whenever the right hand plays the melodic line, the left hand is responsible for taking the bass note and the minim chord (in bars 11 and 13, the right hand joins in by taking the top two notes of the chord), the long notes sustained by pedal. When practising phrase by phrase, it is well worth omitting the melody line and playing the left hand by itself, ensuring accurate measurement in the distances between bass notes and the chords as well as precision in the *legato* pedals (changing pedal on the first beat of each bar). In the left hand, ensure the chord that comes on the second beat is as soft as possible but with all notes sounding clearly. Be sure to preserve the full length of the long melody notes at the changes of pedal (bars 11-12, etc) by observing the ties. Take care that both hands are synchronised to sound precisely together; there is no place for splitting between the hands in this piece.

Grade 7

Group A

Handel   Allegro (from *Suite no. 7 in G minor*, HWV 432)   page 3

George Frideric Handel was born in 1685, the same year as J S Bach and Domenico Scarlatti. A very famous composer in his lifetime, he wrote a number of popular operas, oratorios, and anthems as well as keyboard music. *Allegro* comes from his *Suite no. 7 in G minor* for harpsichord. The movement is in binary form, the first half modulating to the relative major (Bb). The second half passes through two other related keys on the way home (the subdominant in bar 40 and the dominant minor in bar 44), clearly signalled by cadential trills.

When playing Baroque music on the piano it is important to add dynamic variety as well as phrasing and articulation. A solid *f* is a suitable dynamic level for the character at the start, lightening a little in bar 9 and with an echo effect possible in bars 15-16 (there is another similar echo in bars 35-36). A drop to *p* works well for the start of the second half (bar 25), growing to *mp* from bar 29 and then *mf* in bar 33. The return to the home key (bar 45) implies *f*, but within all the suggested dynamic levels it will feel natural to add shaping to the lines with *crescendo-diminuendo* hairpins. Quavers sound best when played lightly detached, but some slurs are possible. A certain amount of overholding in the right hand is stylistically appropriate in places where a melodic line is implied within the figuration. In bars 9 and 10, for example, we might hold on to the first semiquaver of the bar for the length of a crotchet, and the fifth semiquaver to the end of the bar. A brisk tempo is required for performance but a playing at a variety of different speeds in practice is excellent for control and finesse.

Mozart   Minuet in D major, K. 355   page 6

The *Minuet in D* is a late work featuring daring chromaticism and bold dynamic contrasts. For such a short piece it is full of riches and surprises. The texture is in three parts as though conceived in terms of a string trio (with the occasional octave doubling in the upper part and double stops in the middle part). As is customary in a Classical minuet, the form is binary moving from tonic to dominant at the double bar, then back to the tonic by the end.

The given fingering ensures a *legato* between both parts in the right-hand thirds at the start (bars 1-4); balance the sound slightly in favour of the upper voice and aim for precision in sounding the thirds together. Do not be timid with the *sforzandos* (bar 5, etc) yet allow the tension to release in the *p* bar that follows; the left-hand crotchets can be slightly separated here (bar 6, etc). Relax the mood at the codettas (bar 12-16 and 40-44) and lighten the left hand here by playing the quavers in the middle voice detached. The dissonance is most extreme at the beginning of the second half, the *f* at bar 17 should be pronounced. Maintain the tension in the unison passage between bars 24 and 28, relaxing the tempo slightly in the *diminuendo* at bar 28. Savour the varied setting of the opening theme in bar 29. Discreet use of the pedal will assist with some of the awkward joins and provide warmth and resonance to the sound; take care not to blur the lines or cover over phrase endings.

Eberl   Allegro (1st movt from *Sonate*, op. 6)   **page 8**

Anton Eberl was a student of Mozart, a famous touring piano virtuoso and a much-admired composer in his day. Nowadays his music is virtually forgotten, however. The *Sonate in C* is clearly inspired by the orchestra, and a vivid performance will bring out the contrasts not only in dynamics but also in the changes of texture and mood and character between the various themes.

Eberl belonged to a period when the composer indicated those notes that were to be played *legato*. It is up to the performer to decide how to play notes that do not have any articulation marks; in a fast movement such as this they are likely to be detached. All notes in the opening *f* phrase should be separated, the last two crotchets crisply so; the left-hand crotchets in bars 8-9, 28, etc, are also detached. Carefully observe all two-, three- and four-note slurs as well as whole-bar phrases (bar 3, etc) by making the last note softer and slightly shorter. Clarity of texture is paramount, so use the pedal sparingly. By all means add a direct pedal to highlight the *fp* in bar 8, and direct pedals to the chords in bar 20, etc. Light touches may be used for warmth and resonance in the *dolce* second theme (from bar 24) and the codettas (bars 43-49 and 89-95). With Baroque and Classical period works in particular, it is good to practise from time to time without any pedal to keep your sound clear and transparent.

Schytte *ed.* Snell   Etude in A minor, op. 58 no. 6   page 13

Ludvig Schytte was a Danish composer, pianist and teacher of the late Romantic period whose teachers included Niels Gade and Franz Liszt. *Etude in A minor, op. 58 no. 6* is a study in control of right-hand broken-chordal figurations and scale patterns over a left hand that features jumps. The tempo is fairly brisk (*allegretto*) and the character dance-like. The form is ABA, the contrasting middle section in the relative major key of C.

Aim for evenness in the RH semiquavers, maintaining a *legato* as you shape the phrases according to the dynamic markings and the *crescendo-diminuendo* hairpins. Pay careful attention to the fingering, making sure to stick to it each and every time you practise. Once ingrained you will find you will be able to play without thinking about which note or which finger comes next, enabling you to focus on communicating the musical message in performance. Slow practice is an excellent way to begin learning; return to it on occasion thereafter to keep the fingers in shape. You may also find value in practising the semiquavers in a variety of different rhythmic patterns (try a dotted rhythm, then *slow-quick-quick-quick*, etc). The left hand requires care in measuring the distances accurately and freely, and a certain amount of routine separate-hand practice will guarantee success. Judicious use of the pedal is called for throughout; there are two types of pedalling involved, direct and *legato*. In direct pedalling (A sections) the hand and foot go down and come up together; in *legato* pedalling (B section) the foot goes down just after the hand.

J S Bach   Prelude in G major, BWV 860   *Henle*

The *Prelude in G* comes from the first book of Bach's *Well-Tempered Clavier*, an important collection of 48 preludes and fugues in every key; G major was a happy and peaceful key for Bach. The time signature of $^{24}_{16}$ is unusual, indicating all semiquavers are triplets and a tempo that is very light and quick. In keeping with this, a light *staccato* (*leggiero*) touch is suitable in the semiquavers, the quavers being generally crisply detached. The quaver pairs in the RH of bars 11-13 should be played as slurs, since these are *appoggiaturas*. There is a line implied by the first note of each semiquaver group (bars 4 and 5, etc), inviting a slight accent.

This Prelude is built on an underlying harmonic progression that determines how we might shape the piece in performance. The spinning semiquaver patterns in bars 1 and 2, for example, outline the progression I–IV–V^7–I on a tonic pedal (the left hand repeated Gs). It would be worth playing the harmonic outline either in block chords or simply in two voices (bar 4, etc) for the remainder of the piece to reveal the modulations and overall shape. A strong sense of this harmonic structure will assist with a dynamic plan in performance; for example, you will probably feel a *diminuendo* from bar 1 to 2, followed by a hairpin *crescendo-diminuendo* in bar 4 and bar 5. The diminished chord in bar 6 lends itself to a change of dynamic (perhaps *poco forte*), followed by a lightening of energy in the next bar. A *diminuendo* in the descending sequence from bar 11-13 will feel natural; from the low point in bar 14 you might make a gradual *crescendo* to the triumphant end.

Allegro molto

Haydn (3rd movt from *Sonata in C major*, Hob. XVI:50) *Henle*

This is the last movement of the so-called 'English' Sonata in C, inspired by the powerful and resonant Broadwood pianos Haydn encountered on a visit to London in the 1790s. The music is full of humour and lightness of spirit, requiring a sense of comic timing in the *fermatas*. In bar 10, for example, Haydn takes a wrong turning and has to stop for a while to figure out how to get back on track. He carries on as though nothing happened, but he loses his way again in bar 65 and yet again in bar 69. Enjoy teasing your listeners in these places as they scratch their heads wondering what Haydn is playing at.

The tempo is *allegro molto* (very lively). Haydn has marked those notes he wants played *legato* and *staccato*; unmarked crotchets work best when lightly detached. The grace notes are played on the beat; since the notes they connect to are all short a good solution is to play the grace note and the main note simultaneously, touching in the grace note as lightly as possible. Two-note slurs should be carefully articulated, with a break after the second note. Pay close attention to the dynamics, the contrasts between *f* and *p* are important for the character changes. Instead of bringing the movement to a strong close, Haydn writes a throwaway ending (marked *p*) and we feel the music scampering away.

Dabs of pedal add colour and resonance to the accents (the spread chords in bars 38, 51, etc) but use it sparsely and cautiously elsewhere to preserve clarity of texture and articulation.

Mozart Allegro (1st movt from *Sonata in G major*, K. 283) *Henle*

This graceful movement in G major makes almost no use of the minor, except for a short interruption to A minor just after the start of the recapitulation in bar 75; bring out the LH *f* (bars 75 and 79) to highlight the element of surprise. The lyrical first subject is gentle and contented; there is a livelier energy in the transition between first and second subjects (bars 16-22) and it would be unnatural not to respond to the rising sequence here by adding a *crescendo*, so by all means do (Mozart does not write all performance directions in the score, leaving much up to the performer). As is common in first movement sonata form, there are several different ideas in the second subject area – aim to bring a new character to each. There is coyness in the phrase from bar 23-26, the mood changing to playfulness and later exuberance as Mozart heads to the double bar. Make the most of the sudden *p* to *f* contrasts (bar 31, 38, etc).

Quavers that do not have phrase markings or slurs are for the most part non-*legato* (except for the LH from bar 80, which need to supply a harmonic carpet for the RH melody). Give semiquavers passages melodic interest by shaping the lines with *crescendo-diminuendo* hairpins. Ornaments come on the beat, the *appoggiaturas* (bar 37, etc) played as semiquavers. Take care with the pedal; short dabs may be appropriate here and there for resonance but all rests should be clear and audible, and textures clear and transparent. Judicious use of finger pedalling (overholding touch) in the *Alberti* figures (bar 1, etc) adds resonance in the LH while preserving clarity in the RH.

Group B

Mendelssohn	No. 2 from Kinderstücke, op. 72	page 16

Mendelssohn wrote his set of six *Children's Pieces, op. 72* for his young relatives during his summer holiday to England in 1842. No. 2, an *andante sostenuto* in the key of E♭, close in spirit to the composer's many *Songs Without Words*, features a lyrical melody in the right hand supported by gently flowing semiquaver patterns in the left.

After a short introduction based on the tonic and dominant chords the melody appears with the indication *cantabile* (in a singing style). What does this mean for the pianist? Apart from playing the melody more strongly than the accompaniment, we also need to add shaping and shading to the line. Singing it is the very best way to find where the line needs to breathe; you will also discover where the high and low points occur. When you play, aim to replicate the line as though you were singing it. Intervals that are close together are easier to sing (seconds and thirds); those that are further apart may need a little more time to be expressive (give a little more space to the interval of the sixth in bar 9, for example). The left hand needs lightness and delicacy of touch, subtly pointing out the implied bass line (the melodic element in the left hand that underpins the right hand's song) while hiding the repeated notes in between the beats. The left hand, like any good accompanist, needs to accommodate the singing line between phrases as well as helping to move it forwards in moments of intensity (the *crescendo* from bar 14, for example). Beware of interrupting the flow by making a break in sound at phrase ends; a smooth *legato* is called for here.

Turina	Fiesta (from *Miniatures*)	page 18

Fiesta is one of a set of eight pieces entitled *Miniatures* by Spanish composer Joaquín Turina. It makes a very effective recital piece for the intermediate pianist, containing elements of showmanship and display but also calling for imagination and the ability to paint a picture in sound. The Spanish fiesta is an opportunity for people to celebrate by singing, dancing, eating and generally have a good time together in the sunshine, often dressing up in fancy costumes. Researching some images of the fiesta online will certainly put you in the mood to play this piece! *Fiesta* opens with the strumming of a guitar, and soon the dancing starts (bar 11). What is the interruption in bar 15, and what is the singer telling us in bar 23? Is there rain on the way, perhaps? The mood seems to darken here, especially in bars 31-32. Only you can decide what is going on in your story; to help clarify it, you may want to write a paragraph describing it.

The right-hand repeated notes at the start work best with a change of finger on each note as this allows the hand to keep mobile and the arm free. There is some flexibility in the tempo in the right-hand single-line melodies (bars 23-27 and 47-51), otherwise maintain a steady pulse throughout. Careful right-hand practice will help with the awkward chord shapes in bars 11-14 and the descending cascade from bar 39. Beware of over pedalling; short dabs are suitable on each left-hand crotchet from bar 11, etc, and we need to hear the rests in bars 27-28. Whole-bar pedals are effective in bars 45-46 and from 55-58.

Chanler — Aftermath
page 21

Theodore Chanler was an American composer who died in 1961. He is mostly remembered for his songs, but he also wrote an opera, choral music as well as chamber works and music for piano. *Aftermath* was composed in 1942; it is just 21 bars long and has the hallmarks of a song without words in late Romantic style. A successful performance relies on shaping and projecting a melodic line expressively over broken chord patterns, flexibility in timing (*rubato*) and sensitivity to nuance and pedalling.

A two-against-three polyrhythm is featured throughout, with triplets in the left hand and duplets in the right. It is good preliminary practice to master a few scales in this way, in the tempo and style of the piece (remember to start with the hands two octaves apart to avoid a collision). When transferring this skill to the piece approach the triplets with freedom, allowing them to ebb and flow fluidly. As with any piece that has a melodic line, it is always helpful to sing the line first to find out where the breathing places are, and where the high and low point fall. The first note of each of the sighing quaver pairs on the first beats of bars 1–5, etc, is an *appoggiatura* that forms a dissonance with the harmony; play the second note more softly. The climax of the first eight-bar phrase occurs at the highest note, the F♯ (bar 6); the main climax is at bar 13. There is one pedal to each harmony (crotchet beats); longer pedals are required in bar 13 and in the *dolcissimo* (hold the last two beats of the bar in one pedal).

Earl — Lento (2nd movt from *Sonatina*)
page 25

Born in 1951, David Earl is a South African-born pianist and composer resident for many years in the UK. This is the second movement from the *Sonatina*, composed in 2009. The movement is in polyphonic style beginning with three parts but with a fourth making its presence felt from bar 5. It is helpful to think in terms of a string quartet where all the parts are of equal importance within the ensemble. If we voice slightly in favour of the top notes in general it is more because these higher notes are less resonant than the lower notes on the piano, and would be in danger of being overshadowed by them if we played all parts equally. To hear exactly what is happening in the movement, it is helpful to practise each melodic line by itself and then in combination with another; you might also practise omitting one part at a time while playing the others.

Lento tells us to play slowly, giving the music space. Apart from where marked (the rests in bar 2, etc, and commas at the end of bars 16 and 21), avoid a break in sound at the ends of phrases; allow the music to breathe but connect with some pedal. Distinguish between the three levels of soft playing, **pp** (only from bar 26), **p** and **mp**. Pay close attention to the precise lengths of notes. Aim for finger *legato* wherever possible rather than relying on pedal for joins; the pedal is essential for some connections, as well as for warmth and resonance, but beware of covering over rests (the composer has notated these precisely). The movement allows the performer to convey a mood of wistful contemplation. The closing section (from bar 22) might be a touch slower and *lontano*, creating a sense of 'another place, another time'.

Peter-Horas   Sarah

Thomas Peter-Horas was born in Germany in 1959. His piano style is best described as crossover, because it mixes elements of classical, jazz and pop. *Sarah* is in ternary form (ABA) with the climax occurring in the B section (bar 36). The first A section, marked *p*, features a lyrical melodic line over an arpeggiated accompaniment. When the A section returns (bar 45) we find a countermelody underneath the original melody, forming an alto part.

In order to project the melody line clearly above the left hand in the opening section it is helpful to think in terms of two different dynamic levels, thus left hand *p*, right hand *mp-mf*; longer right-hand notes (the tied Fs in bar 5, etc) will need more tone to sustain across the bar line. Maintaining a *legato* in the left hand throughout each two-bar harmonic unit (bars 5-6, etc) will help with tonal control and rhythmic stability. Pedal according to each new harmony, enjoying the build-up of resonance. The first pedal change need only occur on the downbeat of bar 7, then again in bar 9. Because bar 10 is a new harmony a fresh change is necessary on the downbeat; bars 36-37 need one pedal for the two bars in order to sustain the bass octave. Some careful slow practice with the right hand alone will help security as well as tonal control in the final section. Aim to hold the long notes in the right hand from bar 48 where possible and where comfortable; allow the upper voice to sing above the alto line, which needs to be play softly within the overall *mf* dynamic.

Harris   Study   Trinity

Paul Harris' modern take on the traditional study in finger velocity is appealing and inventive. It provides a refreshing alternative to Czerny and Clementi staples, and is really fun to play. Note how this study in C major that veers off into black and white patterns from the first bar, gives both hands an equal workout. Dexterity in the semiquaver passagework and rhythmic precision throughout are basic requirements; no pedal is necessary.

As you practise, aim to identify as many of the tonal centres as you can (for example, the right hand in bar 3 begins with an ascending scale of E major followed by a decorated five-finger position in Bb major). It is fine to play the opening LH quavers with a light detachment and where the semiquavers flow between the hands, observe where these need seamless continuation (eg bars 13 and 15) or contrast (eg bar 6) as the music suggests. Careful control of the final *crescendo* (from bar 16) will help to achieve a sense of elan in the closing bars. If you struggle to play fluently at the required *allegro moderato* tempo, you will find security in practising at a variety of different speeds, starting slowly and always insisting on complete accuracy in notes and fingerings as well as listening for evenness in rhythm at the given dynamic level. Such careful and disciplined work is indispensable for control; many professional pianists find that returning to slow practice even after they have learned the notes helps them maintain a high level of technical command.

Liszt   Klavierstück in E major, R. 60   *Bärenreiter*

The *Klavierstück (Piano Piece) in E* is the first of 5, written in 1865. While the technical demands may seem simple enough on first glance, this piece requires care with pedalling, control of touch and tone in soft and loud dynamics, and a feeling for timing in a very slow tempo.

Liszt instructs us to put down the *una corda* pedal (left pedal) at the start and to hold it there until just before the climax (*tre corde* in bar 30). While there is no direction to use it again when the A section returns in bar 37, you may do so at your discretion. The effect of the soft pedal is to change the timbre of the sound by muting it; it is still possible to play firmly and even quite strongly with the left foot down (the *crescendo* from bar 27). Carefully observe the long (right) pedal markings in the introduction; the *staccato* dots under the slur here and elsewhere (bars 31 and 33) indicate a certain emphasis, played non-*legato* but held in the pedal. In bars 35-36 make the tiniest of separations between the *portato* quavers (the effect is like sobbing or panting). Release the pedal carefully on the resolutions in the right-hand line (the B in bar 6 and the F♯ in bar 8, etc) to avoid smudging the melodic line. In the last two bars, each resolution requires a change of pedal (left hand third beat of bar 44; right hand downbeat of bar 45). The piece is punctuated by rests; enjoy these and make the most of them, remembering that silence can be an important expressive ingredient in music.

Prokofiev   Vision Fugitive no. 10   *Boosey*

Visions fugitives (Fleeting Visions) is a set of short untitled pieces written between 1915 and 1917 by Russian composer Sergei Prokofiev. No. 10, marked *ridicolosamente* does not have an actual tempo but a moderate speed gives the player the opportunity to bring out the quirky, grotesque humour and manage the fast notes without rushing. Perhaps the opening LH music sounds like a machine, and the RH the braying of a donkey (the accents need to be very strong, almost strident)? There is a ludicrous march that starts in bar 11, interrupted by mocking laughter in bar 15 as though the music was poking fun at someone. This is certainly not a polite piece!

A strictly metronomic approach would adversely affect the character as much as playing with exaggerated *rubato*. The secret lies in knowing how to place certain events to underline their rhythmic effect. The downbeat of bar 17, for example, may be played very slightly late. There is room for your own personality here, and no two players will interpret the piece in the same way. The last two bars work just as well with a subtle *ritardando* as with a slight hurrying forwards. Pedal, if used at all, must never affect the dryness of the *staccato* quaver pattern that permeates the piece from start to finish; all *legato* connections must therefore be achieved by hand. *Sotto* (bar 18) tells us that the right hand should be under the left; *sopra* (bar 19) the right hand is now over the left. Play the roulades in bars 15 and 16 (etc) very lightly with clean articulation. Grace notes are played before the beat.

Rocherolle   La Chapelle   *Kjos*

This evocative piece by American pianist and composer Eugénie Rocherolle is beautifully written for the piano, making full use of the pedal to build up sonorities from sustained bass notes and rolling harmonies. It is music from the heart, calling for a romantic spirit and the ability to play freely with *rubato* and plenty of feeling. It makes a very effective recital piece and will be popular with players and listeners alike.

The piece is in two halves, each starting *adagio* and gradually picking up the pace from andante to moderato as the texture thickens and the mood becomes more passionate and expansive. A brief coda returns to *tempo primo* and the hymn-like character of the start. The mood is solemn and reverential yet tender in the two *adagio* sections; allow the quaver movement to help move the music forwards in the *andante* (bars 9 and 30) so that it can build to the climaxes in both *moderato* sections (bars 17 and 38) where the tempo is significantly faster and the feeling joyous. The pedal is your ally when used correctly. To avoid blurs and smudges, make sure to lift the pedal all the way to the top in order to clear all traces of the previous harmony before putting it down again; you will need to be especially attentive to your right foot as the textures thicken. At the *moderato* (bars 17 and 38) take a moment on each new bass note (the first quaver of the bar) to make sure you catch it in the pedal. If you do this well you will build an impressive wave of sound that releases at the end of each RH phrase. You will need to change pedal on each crotchet in bars 8 and 29.

Schubert — Moment Musical no. 6 (Plaintes d'un Troubadour) — Bärenreiter

The title translates as *Complaints of a Troubador*, but it is not Schubert's own. The piece was so named when it made its first appearance in an album of short pieces by various composers published in Vienna in 1824; it later became the final piece in Schubert's set of six miniatures, the *Moments musicaux*. The form is ABA, each section itself in ternary form; the *da capo* repeat after the Trio is mandatory in any performance. One of the hallmarks of Schubert's music is his distinctive use of harmony, allowing his music to move through different tonal regions and often touching on unexpected harmonies on the way. When the music changes to the key of E major in bar 29, the mood seems to change with it; is there a bittersweet feeling here, a sense of longing?

The tempo is *allegretto*, so not too fast. A slow minuet tempo allows the necessary space to underline the many moments of harmonic and textural beauty in performance, and while the piece may not look too difficult at first glance it requires a thoughtful approach in the practice room. An important consideration is achieving a good tonal balance at each dynamic level, from *pp* to *ff* (notice where the dynamic changes are sudden, and where they are prepared by a *crescendo* or *diminuendo*). Chord voicing is another challenge to overcome, requiring very careful listening and experimentation until you find the right blend from all the notes in the chords (rather than projecting a top melody line). The lower notes in both hands from bar 17–20 contribute more to the soundscape than the repeated Cb on the top, for example, and moments of contrary motion between the parts need to be heard clearly (bars 4, 22, 35, etc). Breathe between phrases, and create *legato* by hand wherever possible.

Skulte — Arietta — Peters

Ādolfs Skulte was a Latvian composer and music educator who died in 2000. *Arietta (Little Song)* is in neo-Baroque style requiring a projected singing tone in the RH, a full range of dynamics, sensitivity to phrasing and harmony and good control of the pedal. The tempo is slow, the mood solemn and the character noble.

Think of the top line as though sung by a soprano voice, or played on a violin. The first beat of each bar is marked with a *tenuto*, telling us to give the note more weight; shape the line beautifully by emphasising its high and low points and allowing it to breathe naturally at the ends of phrases. To help you project the melody clearly, the LH needs to be quite a bit softer. However, because there is a lot of interest in the LH it is worth practising it by itself on occasion, savouring the dissonant harmonies and bringing out the slurred quavers expressively, as though sighing (bar 6, etc). Resist the temptation to spread the left-hand chords; all notes need to sound precisely together. Observe all dynamic markings carefully; the challenge is not to play so softly in the *p* at the start that the *pp* in bar 36 cannot be softer. Similarly with the *fortes* on the first page, keep something in reserve for the *ff* at the climax in bar 31. *Legato* pedal is essential in this piece; as a general principle, change on each crotchet beat making sure to listen for the RH rests, which are breathing places.

Tanner — How Bleak the Sea Tonight — Spartan

This atmospheric piece comes from Mark Tanner's *Nightscapes for Piano*. It requires responsiveness to the mood, a vivid imagination and careful control of left hand and pedal.

The hands are placed far apart leaving a big gap in the middle of the texture (a main contributing factor to the bleakness of the title), and the LH is much more active than the RH. Listen very carefully to the LH, aiming for a smooth and even effect in the semiquaver patterns while sensing that each half-bar unit creates a wave (shallow waves in the outer sections but bigger ones in the middle section from bar 11). Important bass notes are marked *tenuto*; give these a little more time not only because of the leaps but also because they add a bass dimension that complements the RH's high treble register and the gulf between the hands. Despite the $\boldsymbol{pp}$ marking the RH will need a certain amount of projection and shine to give it profile. Apart from bars 18 and 19, where a long pedal is marked, we change the pedal twice per bar. This type of long pedalling creates mild dissonance from neighbouring notes that are not part of the harmony, but don't be afraid of this build-up of sound – this gentle mistiness is absolutely what we are after here. In the middle section you may be tempted to change the pedal on the second and fourth beats but resist this at all costs; the marked pedalling creates a lovely effect, allowing a build-up of resonance as the mood becomes more fervent.

Grade 8

Group A

Rameau   Fanfarinette and La Triomphante (from *Suite in A minor*)   page 3

Jean-Philippe Rameau was an important composer and theorist of the High Baroque. In addition to operas and other works for the stage, cantatas and motets, Rameau wrote three books of very fine pieces for harpsichord. *Fanfarinette* and *La Triomphante* come from the *Suite in A minor* (third book), and are examples of character pieces with descriptive or fanciful titles typical of the French style. *Fanfarinette* derives from the word *fanfaron* (meaning 'braggart'), and calls for light and graceful treatment. *La Triomphante* evokes a feeling of triumph and exuberance; experiment with a non-*legato* touch in the quavers and a stronger dynamic ($\boldsymbol{f}$, dropping to a $\boldsymbol{mf}$ after the double bar line). Pedal is best avoided.

The ornaments are much harder to execute on the piano than the harpsichord. Beginning on the beat, they call for considerable delicacy of touch, especially when they occur in both hands simultaneously. The short trills (indicated by the wavy line) conventionally start from the upper note; the minimum requirement is four notes, although you can extend the trill on long notes if desired. For greater ease in execution, a main-note start to the trill has been suggested in some places. When a trill is connected to the previous note by a slur (bar 5, etc) play a three-note ornament starting on the main note (thus main note, upper note, main note).

Bach   Prelude in G major, BWV 902/1   page 6

Bach might well have intended this as the Prelude for Book 2 of the *Well-Tempered Clavier*, instead selecting a shorter and lighter piece that he felt was a better pairing for the G major Fugue. The Prelude is a *galant* style keyboard sonata in binary form with two halves of equal length, featuring part writing alternating with *concertante* scale passages and triplet figuration.

In Bach's day performance decisions were mostly left to the good taste of the individual performer. This piece contains no directions, giving us the freedom to find our own colourful range of phrasing, dynamics and articulation to bring out the character of the music as it unfolds. You might find it helpful to pencil in your ideas as you experiment. But how to decide? There are no absolute rules, only guidelines. When the opening material returns in the dominant key (bar 9), it is natural to play it more strongly. Making a small separation before a syncopation brings out its rhythmic accent; shaping semiquaver patterns with gentle *crescendo-diminuendo* hairpins shows the rise and fall of the line. It feels natural to gain in intensity in note patterns that ascend, getting softer in patterns that descend (try making a very gradual *diminuendo* in the falling sequence from bar 16 to 21, for example). Notes that move stepwise sound better when played more *legato*; those that move in wider intervals can be separated, but avoid a clipped *staccato*. The walking bass quaver lines (bar 11) may be played *legato* or slightly detached, but a mixture of the two is preferable. To preserve clarity of line and texture, the pedal is best avoided.

Haydn   Moderato (1st movt from *Sonata in G minor*, Hob. XVI/44)   page 10

The *Sonata in G minor, Hob XVI/44* was composed in the early 1770s and is an example of the *Empfindsamer Stil* (sensitive style) developed by musicians and poets in 18th century Germany to express true and natural feelings. Sudden changes in mood are a feature of this style, and Haydn uses major and minor contrasts to express dark and light. The key of G minor is associated with sadness and tragedy.

This is one of a number of early sonatas Haydn intended for the harpsichord, which explains why there are no dynamic markings. The harpsichordist achieves colour, contrast and expression by other means; when playing this music on the piano we should feel free to avail ourselves of the resources of the piano by adding our own dynamics and pedalling in ways that are stylistically appropriate. Here are some suggestions. The sudden shift to Bb minor (bar 9) needs a special colour; begin softly and open up the sound to the end of the phrase. A *crescendo* is natural in the ascending sequences (bars 15–17, etc) and implied from bar 46 as the texture thickens when voices enter one after the other. Pedal should never cover articulation markings or clarity of the part writing but we may use small dabs of pedal for colour and resonance (bar 10, 12, etc.). Pay close attention to Haydn's articulation markings. *Staccato* wedges indicate detachment but notes should not be played very short; unmarked quavers may be detached. Play the second note of slurred pairs softer and slightly shorter.

Mozart   Allegro (1st movt from *Sonata in B flat*, K. 570)   page 16

Composed in Vienna in 1789, the *Sonata in B flat, K. 570* is Mozart's penultimate piano sonata and an example of his mature style. During his Vienna decade he had been studying the music of J S Bach, and we see its influence in the contrapuntal elements in the *Sonata* (the second theme at bar 41, for example).

The movement opens with a very simple theme featuring the notes of the tonic chord in minims and crotchets. It is easy to begin too quickly; feel the quaver rhythm from bar 5 before you start to ensure stability of the pulse from the outset. The long *legato* line is not part of eighteenth century style, and we notice how many short, articulated phrases Mozart indicates throughout this movement. In his piano music Mozart borrowed markings from string playing; thinking of a change of bow at the end of a phrase produces a more natural result than making too obvious a gap in sound. In the opening slurred pairs (bars 1–3, etc) play the crotchets lightly, but should we separate them from the minims? A slight separation is perfectly fine, but certainly not a short *staccato*. What about the slurs over the six quavers in bars 5 and 6, etc, and the short semiquaver groups (bar 12, etc)? If it feels choppy, overly fussy or downright impossible to break at the ends of each phrase at the *allegro* tempo we can achieve an authentic effect by instead stressing the first note of each slur or phrase followed by a slight *diminuendo* to the end of it. A carefully organised fingering and sensible practice at a slow tempo will lead to optimal control of the semiquaver passagework, which needs melodic shaping for expressive effect.

Allegro assai
C P E Bach   (1st movt from *Sonata in A major*, WQ 55 no. 4)   *Breitkopf*

Carl Philipp Emanuel Bach was the second son of Johann Sebastian Bach; in addition to his compositions and theoretical writings he was a leading keyboard player of the day. He wrote much music for his favourite keyboard instrument, the clavichord (an instrument, though soft in volume, capable of considerable expressive variety). *Sonata no. 4* was composed in 1765 and published as one of a set suitable for 'connoisseurs and amateurs'. From the strong block chords and brilliant scales to the delicate arpeggios passed between the hands and the virtuosic tremolos and broken intervals, Bach celebrates the keyboard in the most imaginative and exciting way.

The performer needs to revel in the contrasts in dynamics and texture, making the most of the colour possibilities of the different registers of the keyboard. Notice how much variety Bach brings to the descending harmonic progression from bars 4-7 when he repeats it in bars 8-12. The tempo marking is *allegro assai* (very fast), but avoid the temptation to run before you can walk. The greatest security in performance will come after a certain amount of patient and detailed work at a much slower speed, one that allows you to concentrate on every expressive detail (including phrase shaping) while insisting on complete evenness in and control of the semiquaver passages with a fingering that has been carefully chosen and written in the score. Ornaments in this period begin on the beat, and short trills and turns start on the upper note. Short dabs of pedal, if done unobtrusively, add accent and resonance to f chords.

Beethoven   Prestissimo (Finale from *Sonata op. 10 no. 1*)   *Henle*

The last movement from the *Sonata op. 10 no. 1* is in sonata form with a very short development section indeed (bars 46-56). You will notice the similarities between this development section and the Fifth Symphony, worth listening to not only for this reason but also because a knowledge of Beethoven's orchestral music deepens your understanding of his style. The key of C minor was significant for him, and he chose it for some of his most turbulent and dramatic music. The mood is anxious and nervous at the start, but the second theme (from bar 17) much more confident and almost jovial. The right-hand tremolos (from bar 28) are measured, played as semiquavers; organise the turns (bar 4, etc) rhythmically so they do not trip you up.

The *alla breve* time signature instructs us to feel two beats in a bar and not four; in order to gain full technical control at the *prestissimo* marking, a certain amount of careful slow practice observing all of Beethoven's dynamic and articulation markings will prove invaluable. You can build up speed gradually, or by practising short units of just a few notes (half and then whole bars) at a time at full speed. No amount of slow practice will solve the challenging three-against-four polyrhythm (bars 34-35); it is very constructive to accent those notes that coincide between the hands during practice, but in performance listen carefully to the left hand and let it be your conductor. Relax the tempo just before the coda (bar 106). Beethoven restates the second at a slower tempo, in the key of D♭ major (the flattened second degree in the key of C, a relationship known as the Neapolitan). After one final angry outburst in bar 114, the movement ends softly, in a whisper.

Chopin — Waltz in E minor, op. post. — *Henle*

This scintillating waltz was written around 1830 and is an excellent recital piece, demanding of the player lightness of touch as well as bravura. It is in modified ternary form with an introduction and coda; the middle section (from bar 57) is in the bright key of E major.

A change of finger on each repeated note in the main theme (bar 9, etc) helps keep the hand mobile and free. The left hand requires dexterity in measuring the leaps accurately; pay careful attention to *staccato* and slurred notes, playing the second note of each slurred pair shorter. Play all grace notes (bar 11, etc) before the beat. Direct pedal is appropriate for the first section – the right foot goes down with the hands on the first of the bar and comes up on the third beat; there will be a tiny gap in sound over the bar line, which adds the necessary punctuation and rhythmic vitality. In bar 25 there is a change of mood to an expressive *cantabile* style, marked *dolce e legato*. For the sudden *f* from bar 33 play the bass notes on the first beats firmly, catching them in the pedal. Don't be squeamish about pedalling through bars 73 and 75 for the full *ff* effect; the short-lived dissonance from the LH chromatic notes will not have a chance to offend. Despite the slurs over the LH in bars 89–95 the touch is *leggiero* and very soft. A dramatic diminished seventh chord rudely interrupts the return of the A section (bar 108) and plunges us into the coda. Notice the two long pedal markings (bars 113–116 and 123–127); the effect is an exciting build-up of resonance. Rests in the latter example should not be taken as literal silences, rather that nothing is played on these beats.

Handel — Presto (final movt from *Suite no. 3 in D minor*, HWV 428) — *Henle*

The *Presto* is the last movement from the *Suite in D minor*, originally written for the harpsichord. As a tempo direction *presto* in the Baroque period is not as fast as it came to be in later periods, so do not take the tempo too fast. The piece is in binary form and made up of two contrasting ideas, a motive built from solid chords evoking a *tutti* orchestral effect and a second motive in two parts, featuring running semiquavers supported by a quaver bass line. The character is grand in the opening, and a strong *forte* dynamic is implied. There is no need to aim for *legato* connections in the chords – separate each chord from the next and allow the music to breathe between each short phrase. You might even introduce a subtle *allargando* in bar 9 and 10, etc. Drop down to *mf* in the two-part texture from bar 11, adding hairpin contours and phrasing to the RH semiquavers while keeping the LH quavers detached. A softer dynamic is effective at the start of the second half (bar 64), building gradually as the music returns to the opening material in bar 92 (this time in the relative major key of F). You may find it effective to broaden the tempo slightly in the preceding bar (bar 91, and in the parallel bars, 55 and 144), detaching the last few semiquavers if this helps you give due rhythmic emphasis.

Ornaments come on the beat, the trills starting on the upper note. Measure the trills rhythmically, in demisemiquavers. In the case of trills with written-out terminations (bar 1, etc), there should be eight notes in all (six for the trill plus two for the termination). Trills without terminations have a minimum of four notes, but play more repercussions if you wish.

Hengeveld   Prelude (from *Partita Rhythmique*)   *Trinity*

There is a strong influence of J S Bach in the textures and note patterns in this good-humoured *Prelude* from Gerard Hengeveld's *Partita Rhythmique*. Jazz rhythms and harmonies give a twentieth century complexion to the neo-baroque foundations.

Play the opening page somewhat freely, in the spirit of a toccata-like improvisation. Create a seamless continuity as you pass the semiquaver line back and forth between the hands; the LH D♯ in bar 4 is an important arrival point on the journey to the dominant key. Do not misread the rests in bar 10, these simply tell us the lower parts play nothing until the syncopation in the middle of the bar; the semibreve chord on the first beat can only be sustained by the pedal (one long pedal from bar 9–11 is the best solution). From bar 12, all unslurred LH quavers are *staccato*, but firm and not too short. Set a steady tempo and avoid the tendency to rush. Rhythmic buoyancy is more important than speed, the LH providing a sturdy support for the semiquaver movement in the RH. Aim for complete evenness in the semiquaver patterns while responding to the contours of the line and giving it shape. Pedal may be added in the introduction, also in bar 32 and in the coda (from bar 59). Exaggerate all accents, especially when they add zing to syncopations (bar 26, etc) or where they stabilise the pulse in one hand when the other is playing off the beat (bar 31, etc). There is a strong sense of structure in the piece and awareness of these points will help create an effective performance.

Group B

Brahms   Intermezzo in B minor, op. 119 no. 1   page 24

In 1893, Brahms wrote his last work for the piano, a set of four piano pieces, op. 119. The *Intermezzo in B minor* is the first piece of the set. *Intermezzo* is a generic title for a short stand-alone character piece; despite its brevity, this piece has aroused keen interest in composers and scholars as they have striven to analyse it bar by bar. As a composition it is full of riches. Can you discern the key in the first three bars, or find a clear cadence in the home key in the first section (to bar 16)? The middle section in the relative major (D) is less ambiguous and dissonant harmonically, warmer and lighter in spirit with a gentle waltz feeling. The mood in the outer sections is melancholic, wistful and reflective. *Intermezzo* requires an ability to play expressively at a very slow tempo, a feeling for ebb and flow within the pulse (*rubato*), warmth of tone and control of texture and pedalling.

Pay close attention to the part writing throughout the piece and the precise lengths of notes. The texture needs to be controlled carefully at the start so as to project the top melody, making a *diminuendo* in the downward spread chords. Practise the opening (and especially from bar 43) without pedal at first before adding it in discreetly (you can be more lavish with pedal in the second section and the coda). Enjoy the dialogue between the upper voice (violin) and the lower (cello) from bar 12, keeping the offbeat semiquavers in the middle very soft. Allow the left thumb to bring out the hemiola (bars 23-24), and to emerge at the climax (bars 37-38).

Debussy   Minstrels (from *Préludes Book 1*)   page 27

Debussy wrote two books of *Préludes*, revealing the title only at the end of each work. *Minstrels* is the final number from Book 1, and one of his most humorous pieces. A successful performance relies on vivid response to the quick changes of mood, careful observance of all the performances details the composer has marked meticulously in the score, and the ability to tell a story from the imagination. In the early nineteenth century the servants of American plantations put on minstrel shows, the tradition eventually reaching Europe by about 1900. Debussy depicts such a song and dance act, with plenty of comic touches. We hear the banjo, castanets, fiddle and tambourine and the mixture of jazz, ragtime and blues elements. There is tap dancing (bar 9), a sentimental song (bar 63), as well as comic acrobatics throughout.

Rubato and timings are built in (*cédez* tells us to slow down; *serrez* means get faster). Constantly work on control of touch, paying special attention to accents (> and ∧ markings call for a sharp attack; lean on the *tenuto*s and make them heavy). In bars 37–38 find a way of differentiating between the dry *staccato* in the left hand and the longer *mezzo staccato* in the right. Experiment by adding a dab of pedal to accented *staccato* notes and chords to give resonance (the F♯ in bar 1, the chords in bar 18, for example), otherwise use pedal very sparsely in the dry opening section. Even though it is much more convenient to play the right-hand *gruppetti* (grace notes) before the beat (bar 1, etc), Debussy instructs us to play them on the beat. This slightly delays the notes of the theme in relation to the pulse and creates a clownish swagger in keeping with the character.

Ireland   Elegy (from *A Downland Suite*)   page 32

John Ireland wrote *A Dowland Suite* in 1932, originally as a collection of four pieces for brass band. He later arranged some movements for string orchestra and also for piano. An elegy is a sad or sombre piece, often a lament for the dead. The style is in the English pastoral tradition, with a feeling of nostalgia for bygone days.

Control of sound in the thick chordal texture relies on tonal balance and skilful pedalling. Each chord needs to be voiced so that some notes are brought to the foreground, others lightly shaded in. This is harder to achieve in the louder dynamic levels when piano sound is likely to coarsen; remember that in *f* and *ff* some notes within chords might actually be rather soft! Pedal with each change of harmony, except where we find a long bass that can only be sustained by the foot (bar 6, 14, 31, etc). In the spread chords, aim to catch the lowest note in the pedal. Most spreads will sound best before the beat; some might work better on the beat (meaning they can be rolled up slower). To avoid an ungainly break in the line in bar 8, hold on to the right-hand notes as you change pedal on the grace note bass E♭. Do not worry if the occasional non-harmonic tone in upper parts gets caught by the pedal. In bar 10, for example, the long bass note (semibreve) needs to be held in the pedal despite the changing harmonies above. If the inner parts are played more lightly this will not cause offence. In other instances, hold on to long notes by hand where possible so that these notes are sustained when changing the pedal (the long octave F in the left hand in bars 19 and 20, for instance).

Bartók   Allegretto (1st movt from *Suite*, op. 14)   page 34

Much of Bartók's solo piano music is inspired by Eastern European folk music. While the *Suite, op. 14* (1916) is based on original themes we still feel the folk elements strongly – irregular rhythms, simple melodies and exotic scales. We also find the whole-tone scale (from bar 106), which serves to destabilise the feeling of a tonal centre. Bartók moves away from the heavy chordal style of late Romantic piano writing in favour of sparser, simpler and more transparent textures. The opening vamp gives the impression we are going to be in B♭ major, but the music does not settle there. Instead, Bartók explores the connection between B♭ and the remote triad of E (bar 6, etc), making a feature of the blue note (the false relation between major and minor third). Elsewhere we find the melody notes harmonised unexpectedly as the music slips and slides from one seemingly unrelated chord to another. The mood is playful and the character dance-like.

A well-organised fingering is necessary to avoid clashes between the two hands when they are close together in the middle section. Experiment with which hand goes over and which under, recognising that this may switch over suddenly (between bars 71 and 72, for instance, when the right hand moves under the left). Carefully observe all slurs and *staccatos*, and distinguish between the different types of accent (*tenutos* should be played with weight, ^ accents are stronger than > ones). The composer has marked all details of timing and *rubato* carefully in the score.

Ma/Zhang N
arr. Zhang Z   Remote Xianggelila   page 38

This is an arrangement for piano of a Chinese folk melody. Xianggelila is a more recent spelling of the mythical utopia Shangri-La, now a city in northwestern Yunnan province, People's Republic of China.

The music is in the style of a nocturne, and will sound best if we approach it objectively and allow it to speak for itself naturally without romanticising it or overlaying it with too much *rubato* (other than the changes in tempo that are marked in the score). The tempo is a relaxed four in a bar, with no sense of hurry. Float the RH melody over the gentle LH accompaniment, which needs to be in the background throughout. The pedal is responsible for blending notes together into satisfying clouds of harmony and you will discover there is nothing offensive whatever to the ear in catching passing notes and neighbouring melody notes in the long pedals. Enjoy the build-up of resonance and change on each new bass note on the first beat of the bar. Exceptions to this rule are bars 18 and 19, where the pedal may be held for two bars; bars 24 to 26, where half-bar pedals would be appropriate; and in bar 29 pedal with each new bass note (stems down). At the *Lento* (bar 32) pedal according to the harmonies, and enjoy the long pedal for the final three bars. The dynamic range is understated, *mf* being the strongest (the climax at bar 28). Grade the softer dynamics so there is a difference between *ppp*, *pp*, *p* and *mp*.

Grieg   Erotik (from *Lyric Pieces* book 3, op. 43)   *Peters*

Norwegian composer Edvard Grieg wrote 66 miniatures for the piano with the collective title, *Lyric Pieces*. *Erotik* comes from the third book. The direction *lento molto* (very slowly) gives us permission to extract every ounce of expression from melodic lines and juiciness from the harmonies; in each bar there are opportunities for the player to create magical moments. Exaggerate all expressive details, leaning on the *tenuto* notes (bar 1, etc), possibly lingering over the grace notes (bar 2, etc). Many spread chords may be played in a leisurely manner, savouring the luxury and fullness they bring to the texture; organise them carefully so as to capture the bass note with the new pedal, avoiding breaking the melody line. Breathe at the ends of phrases but connect with the pedal so there are no gaps in sound (except in bar 32, where a rest is written). In bar 8 (etc), the left hand crosses over the right to take the melody note. It is perfectly acceptable to use the left pedal (*una corda*) if you wish, even though this is not indicated specifically; it will add a subdued colour to your sound, ideal for the *pianissimo* section (bars 9-16) and at the end.

The stretto marking in bar 18 tells us to get faster; allow the music to move forwards ever more directly (*più mosso e sempre stretto*) to the main climax at bar 27, at which point the music relaxes before the A section returns (the texture now thickened by more activity in the middle parts). Make the most of the *ritardando molto*, and feel the music gradually ebbing away as we reach the end.

Kallmeyer   Six-Eight-Prelude   *DVfM*

This Prelude comes from a collection of easy to moderate piano pieces in different popular idioms, *Cool Cat Piano Goodies* by German composer Ulrich Kallmeyer. The mood is relaxed, possibly a little lazy. There is quite a lot going on in the LH as it jumps from the upper register to the lower in the A section, all of which needs to be done with a light touch. The pedal is responsible for holding many of the LH dotted crotchets (the first beat of bar 3, etc), and a good general pedal plan is to make a *legato* change on each of the two main beats of the bar. If the RH melody is firmly projected and the LH played at a softer dynamic level this will work well. Phrase ends should be tapered off but a break in the *legato* would sound stilted; ensure a *legato* fingering in right-hand phrases. Do not take *staccato* notes too literally in bars 8 and 26 – play short but still within the pedal. However, a break in sound is effective punctuation at the climax, just before the downbeats of bars 28 and 29, and on the low Gs towards the end.

In the B section (from bar 11) we find a different texture; the RH moving up and down the keyboard in decorated arpeggio patterns. When you practise the RH alone, do so at the given dynamic levels (*p* and *pp*), responding to the hairpins. If you prefer a cleaner texture in the B section you may experiment with more frequent pedal changes – on each of the *tenuto* notes, for instance. Enjoy the cross rhythm the LH dotted quavers create. To hold it all together we need to clearly feel two dotted crotchet beats per bar.

Reger   Moment Musical in C sharp minor, op. 44 no. 5   *Peters*

Max Reger was a German composer of the late Romantic period; in addition to large-scale works for piano he wrote a substantial amount of excellent material for teaching purposes. The *Moment Musical* (from a set of *Ten Little Pieces*, op. 44) presents the player with an enigma: how to use the sustaining pedal in the presence of rests and indications to play *staccato*. We need to remember two things about the pedal at the advanced level. Firstly, we do not need to put our foot all the way down to benefit from the added warmth and resonance that even a tiny dab of pedal supplies to our sound; secondly, that articulation and touch is discernable through the pedal. We should of course begin our work with a literal observance of the composer's precise note lengths, obeying the numerous and varied articulation markings before experimenting with how best to add the pedal afterwards. Notice how the soft pedal (*una corda*) not only helps us to play more softly but (on a well-regulated piano) changes the tone colour producing a veiled, muted effect. *Tre corde* instructs us to lift the soft pedal. Those who are averse to using the soft pedal would do well to remember that all pianos from the smallest upright to the largest grand are equipped with this device; it has been present since the invention of the piano, and it is there to be used.

There is a wide range of dynamics, from *ppp* to *ff*, featuring sudden changes from one dynamic level to another. *Anmutig, etwas lebhaft, doch nicht zu sehr* tells us to play 'gracefully, somewhat lively, but not too much'. *Sostenuto* (bar 38) indicates a *rallentando*. In order not to disturb the flexibility of pulse and timings (*rubato*) the piece demands, metronome practice is best avoided.

Schumann   Herberge (from *Waldszenen*, op. 82)   *Wiener UT*

Herberge is the sixth piece from a set of nine short pieces entitled *Waldszenen* (Forest Scenes), written in 1848–49. This was Schumann's last major cycle for piano. There is a warm and friendly atmosphere in this piece; we can almost feel the fire crackling in the grate (the dotted rhythms in bar 3, etc), a welcoming feeling after a day spent hiking through the forest. The tempo is moderate, with opportunities to relax here and there (*etwas zurückhaltend* tells us to hold back slightly; *etwas langsamer* to play somewhat slower). In addition to these places marked by the composer, there are a few other corners that need to breathe (bars 18 and 38, for example). The big chord in bar 43 needs space; smaller hands will need to spread it but this is effective in any case. There is a beautiful moment to savour in bar 25; it is as though the LH were now going to have the chance to play the main melody, only for the RH to snatch it back again in the following bar.

Do not break the line when you find notes marked *staccato* with *tenuto* (bar 2, etc); these markings add emphasis to the notes. When we find *staccatos* under a slur (bar 19), we play half way between *legato* and *staccato* but we may certainly still use touches of pedal. Allow the pedal to catch and sustain the bass notes written as *acciaccaturas* (bars 20, 48 etc). Play all dotted quaver-semiquaver rhythms very sharply, and ensure the triplets in bars 46 and 52–54 are played rhythmically within the pulse.

Sculthorpe   Snow, Moon and Flowers   *Faber*

Peter Sculthorpe was one of Australia's leading composers. *Snow, Moon and Flowers* is the opening piece in a set of three entitled *Night Pieces*. As the composer writes in his preface, the piece 'is based on a Japanese concept known as *setsugekka*, which means, literally, "snow, moon and flowers". This concept is concerned with metamorphosis; moonlight, for instance, may make snow of flowers, and flowers of snow; and the moon itself may be viewed as an enormous snowflake or a giant white flower.'

This music requires extremely careful listening and experimentation with sound as you practise. Tone colour, atmosphere and sensitivity of touch are all-important, especially as the piece calls for great delicacy in many places, and imagination throughout. Carefully observe all the markings in the score; tempo, dynamics, types of accent and pedal are scrupulously indicated by the composer. Distinguish between *tenuto* accents (heavier) and > accents (sharper, more sudden). In *Snow*, notes in the lower stave are taken by the left hand; notes in the upper stave by the right. Give plenty of space at the climax of each movement (marked *molto rall.*), observing that the dynamic level rises only to *mf* in the first two, and *f* in the last (bars 16–18). At first glance the composer's instructions in *Moon* and *Flowers* may look confusing; long pedal marks but with different types of *staccato* and *tenuto* instructions, as well as rests. Remember that touch and articulation can still be heard through the pedal, whose role is to add a misty blanket of resonance around the sound.